Divine
Soldier

Jennifer L. Nelson

Divine Soldier: His Sacrifice, Her Strength

Copyright © 2019 by Jennifer Nelson

DEDICATION

To every man, woman, and child who serves behind a wounded veteran.
Your life has a Godly mission, and you are a mighty warrior. May God bless you and strengthen you as you fight through each challenge, be it spiritual warfare, mental fatigue, or the emotional strain that most will never understand. I pray you will climb your mountain with grit and with encouraging company at your side.

CONTENTS

"Her husband can trust her, and she will greatly enrich his life."
Proverbs 31:11

1

SEVENTEEN AND PRETTY

"You have captivated my heart. ... You hold it hostage with one glance of your eyes."
Song of Solomon 4:9

I never intended to marry a soldier—much less to become a soldier of sorts myself. Yet that is the very path on which I walk. And, in spite of everything, I would not choose a different route. It became, I now can see, an essential part of transforming me from the uncertain girl I was into the on-mission warrior God designed me to be.

I met Nathan Nelson, now my husband of ten years, when I was only seventeen. Back then, his joining with the military was not even on *his* radar. A schoolmate of mine, our mutual acquaintance, was hosting a house party while her parents were out of town. And when I first saw Nathan and a guy I'd later come to know as his friend Colin walk into that Arkansas house, I was dancing with a gal pal. What I remember best about that moment was that everything and everyone simply faded away as I stared at him. I couldn't help myself.

Clearly a little older than me, Nathan was tall and broad shouldered. He was wearing dark jeans and an untucked blue and white pinstripe shirt with its top two buttons undone. He was thin but muscular and walked with a confident sway that charmed me. And I couldn't help but notice that when he smiled at his friend, his entire face scrunched up, turning his eyes into happy slits under his prominent brow. Before the night was over, I'd decide those eyes resembled two beautiful azure gems against his fair skin. In those first moments, though, I felt incredibly shy. Certain that he would see right past me and give attention to one of the other girls at the party.

Prior to that night, I'd never had the self-confidence to talk to boys who caught my interest. And while I had guy friends, I wasn't the kind of girl who expected attention from males in general. Rather, I felt socially awkward, had a tendency to be boisterous, and knew my laughter was loud. I was certain that while some girls deserved to be called "hot," I was better described as merely pretty—if that. And that's why I couldn't believe it and had to coach myself to play it cool when my instant crush soon sauntered over my way, shifting his shoulder-length hair back and out of his face.

"I don't believe we've met," he said in a drawling baritone that I'd come to describe as molasses dripping from a mason jar. "I'm Nathan."

He was so handsome up close that it took my breath away, and I felt my heart flutter. "I'm Jennifer, but my friends call me Jenny," I squeaked.

At this he gave that wonderful smile I'd seen when he entered the room, and I couldn't believe it was all for me. That he was standing there at all seemed surreal. He asked if I went to one of the local high schools, and I admitted that I knew the party hostess through our work on the last theatre production at Jonesboro High. He told me that he worked at Lazzarri's, the Italian restaurant owned by her family. Then he introduced me to his friend Colin and continued to make small talk—apparently every bit as smitten with me as I was with him.

I quickly decided as we stood there that the guy could have just read the back of a cereal box aloud and made it sound sexy. But Nathan's voice had nothing on his face. Square and chiseled, it was the face of a model. (In fact, I'll always consider him the handsomest man I've ever encountered.)

Soon, to my delight, we were dancing together. As hits of the nineties played in the background, he confirmed that I was a junior at Jonesboro, and I learned that he was taking a gap year off of college after one semester at Ole Miss. Before I knew it, we'd spent the evening chatting and laughing and had grown so comfortable with each other that he twirled me about in our friend's kitchen as if we were doing a choreographed number in a movie.

"You have to be the prettiest girl I've ever met," he said as the night drew to a close.

I rolled my eyes at that. "I bet you say that to all the girls."

He denied it, commenting that Colin was always more adept at picking up the ladies.

Shyly, I blushed and gave him my number, which he'd requested earlier. I certainly hoped he wasn't a player because I knew I'd become putty in Nathan Nelson's hands.

What torture that led to as the next three days passed without so much as one phone call for me! As I headed out to cheer at a football game on the evening of that third day, I sorrowfully decided my number must've fallen out of Nathan's pocket or gotten washed away in a laundry accident. Defeated, I began to wonder whether I'd only imagined his interest.

But that night, as I stood in my black and gold cheerleading uniform on the Jonesboro High sidelines and called out our "L-E-T-S-G-O" cheer, I saw him. Nathan Nelson, again with his sidekick Colin, was walking down the bleachers toward the field. (I'd later learn that he'd called just after I left for the game, and my brother—bless him—told him where to find me.) Nathan caught my eye with a wave, and I smiled brightly in acknowledgment of his presence. Just knowing he was up in the stands observing made my emotions flip right along with me as I did my tumbling routine.

At half time I walked over to the fence line, and Nathan was quick to meet me there. Feeling half shy yet totally delighted to see him again, I teased, "Don't you have something more fun to do than attend a high school football game?"

He stepped closer, the picture of confidence. "I tried to call this pretty awesome girl earlier to ask her to dinner, but heard she was here, so I came to find her. What are you doing after the game?"

I said some of the girls and I planned to go grab a bite at Munchies Deli afterward. And to this he replied after a moment of thoughtful silence, "So, how 'bout it?"

"How 'bout what?" I asked, not yet aware that this was Nathan's go-to phrase for many things.

"Can you and I hang out after the game?"

For a long moment his question rang in my mind, and I couldn't even answer him. I just stood staring into those dreamy blue eyes of his, feeling like I'd just won the grand prize on *The Price is Right*. "Sure," I finally said, "but I'll have to ask my folks if it's ok."

He grinned, and we'd both later say that in that moment we each felt as if we were the only two people in the world.

Half time drew to a close, and I hurried to get back in formation. Kate, my petite, blonde teammate, cast a glance at me as we stood side by side with our hands behind our backs to watch the players get into position on the field. She said, "Who was that super-hot guy you were talking to, Jenny?"

I told her with a smile, careful not to draw our coach's attention by turning my head away from the action or talking too loudly. "He's pretty dreamy, right?"

"Well, don't look behind you now," she teased, "but Mr. Nathan Nelson hasn't taken his eyes off *you* from the moment you parted."

I couldn't help myself. I covertly glanced over my shoulder and up into the stands. Sure enough, Nathan sat watching me. Smiling at me. And I gave a flirty smile right back.

While the remainder of the game unfolded, I followed coach's calls and gave every appearance that I was mentally committed to whatever was happening as my school's Hurricanes fought Nettleton's Raiders. But inwardly, I was in knots. Technically, I still wasn't allowed to date. Historically, my parents had kept such a tight rein on me that I knew I'd probably find more support from them were I to announce that I was becoming a nun than if I told them an older guy had just asked me out and tried to enlist their permission for joining him. Their daughter was a good girl, raised in church and well sheltered, and they intended to keep me that way.

Looking back, I appreciate their efforts. I think, though, that observing the strength of marriages built on biblical principles and hearing the testimonies of people who'd chosen virginity until marriage did a lot more to shape my early views on dating and purity than all the hedges Mom and Dad erected around me ever could've. That fall, it was important to me to save some things for my honeymoon; I felt like doing so was an investment I could make in my own future, and I liked that thought. My folks could've saved themselves a lot of stress—and me a lot of frustration—had they just trusted me.

By the time the band started playing "Rock You Like a Hurricane" and the bleachers emptied, I'd come to the sad conclusion that as excited as I was over the prospect of going on a date with the handsomest guy I'd ever seen, my parents were likely to refuse even to let me go to Munchies if Nathan were tagging along. And I couldn't imagine them allowing us to go anywhere alone.

I wasn't surprised, then, when Mom soon said, "I certainly didn't miss seeing that very attractive boy talking to you, Jen, but I just don't think it's a good idea for you to go running around town with some young man we haven't even met."

Dad agreed. "If he wants to see you, he needs to talk to me." Then he proceeded to go on and on about how a nice young man would know the importance of picking up a lady at her parents' house, like a gentleman. And when I tried to tactfully suggest that it might be time to revisit that rather antiquated notion, he made that announcement I'd long since come to hate: "You live in our house; you follow our rules." I knew that was the end of the discussion.

Feeling more like a toddler than a young woman, I made my way to Nathan and gave him the embarrassing news. To my immense relief, he didn't seem rattled. He nodded, almost as if he'd expected that hurdle, and asked for my address. Then he smiled gently, asking, "Dinner and a movie tomorrow? I'd pick you up at six. How 'bout it?"

Blushing, both from humiliation that my parents had interfered with his original plan and because I was so attracted to the guy I feared I might swoon, I nodded.

Saturday arrived and with it came a host of questions. "How did you meet this boy?" Mom asked. I took care with my response. "How old is he?" Dad wanted to know. The two years of difference in our ages might just as well have been twenty. "And what was his excuse for not going straight into the next semester of college?" they both asked several times. Nothing I said could soothe their concerns on that point. As the day wore on, it became increasingly clear my parents were deeply aggravated that a nineteen-year-old boy wanted to take their seventeen-year-old daughter out at all. But what was worse was their stated assumption that he was a partier who had flunked out of school and tried to cover his laziness with some story about a gap year. As the clock ticked toward six, I began to doubt they'd let me go out with him even though he'd agreed to do things their way.

I took a deep breath when the doorbell chimed: Nathan had arrived a few minutes early. Dad opened the door for him and seemed a bit rattled when my date had to duck slightly to avoid hitting his head on the doorframe.

"You sure are a tall fella," Dad commented, his tone making it obvious to me that he saw Nathan's six-foot-one frame as another strike against him.

Nathan was cordial and friendly, but my parents came at him with all the suspicion the FBI would aim at a known convict in disguise. Mom even started trying to play the dreaded "Twenty Questions" game with him, as if in doing so she could sniff out some horrible defect in his character or background: "Where are you from? What do your parents do? Do you have siblings? And tell us again—I didn't quite understand—just why aren't you in college?"

As far as I was concerned, they might just as well have welcomed him into our home by placing him in front of a firing squad. But Nathan proved himself to be a champ, tactfully dodging every trap with ease. He was polite and kind and answered each question with honesty and confidence.

Finally, though, I couldn't take anymore. "I think we are going to be late for the movie if we don't go."

Nathan glanced down at his watch and nodded in agreement. To my parents he said, "It's very nice to meet you both. What time should I have her home?"

"Nine thirty," Dad said sternly.

But by that time, we were nearly a half hour into our date and had yet to cross town to see a film that wouldn't start until 7:15. I explained my concerns. Dad had, after all, already given Nathan his grudging approval to our dinner and a movie plan by then.

After hearing me out, Dad looked Nathan in the eye, essentially staring him down. "Okay, then. Be back by eleven and not a minute after. I will be standing at this door waiting."

"Yes, sir," Nathan said, and we turned to go.

"And another thing," Dad barked behind us. "Keep in mind I have a shotgun *and* a shovel. They'll find you if you hurt her."

Nathan turned back to him, wide eyed. I wanted to fall through the floor. "Yes sir," he said after a moment. "I assure you both she's in safe company."

After that, my date and I walked out to the car and I felt my shoulders relax. I giggled to see that Nathan drove the exact same year, model, and make of vehicle that I did: a ninety-three, gold Toyota Camry. *His and hers,* I thought. It seemed like a good omen. He opened the car's door for me before walking around to the driver's side and sending a pleasant goodbye to my parents. They had decided to stand out on the porch to watch us depart.

"I am so incredibly sorry," I said as Nathan started the car and backed out of the driveway.

"For what?"

"They were rude to you. Besides, we don't even own a shotgun."

Nathan chuckled and took a quick glance my way as he put the car into drive. "Jenny, if I had a daughter that looked like you, I would sit on the sofa and clean my gun while staring a hole through any guy who came by."

My heart stuttered at the earnestness of his words. Even more compelling were the next ones: "You really are beautiful. I'd be happy to let your parents grill me for hours just to have a few moments with you."

The night passed in a wonderful blur. I felt so lucky to be in Nathan's company! At the theatre, he bought us popcorn and a soda to share. Then we watched a comedy that would become one of our favorites, providing many one-liners that we'd quote often. As we sat side by side, it delighted me to realize that when my date laughed, his shoulders shook. In fact, his laugh was so infectious that a few times I giggled along with him and forgot to pay attention to the film.

I was famished by the time the credits rolled. Nathan suggested we go to a little family-owned place called Dixie Cafe, and as we slid into a booth, sitting across from one another, he grabbed the menu and said, "Order anything you want." I distinctly remember thinking, as I looked over the selections, that though I was really hungry, I didn't want to seem like a pig lining up to the trough. I also didn't want to be an expensive date. So, I ordered chicken tenders and fries and smiled when he, whether to assure me he could afford it or because he was just as hungry as I, ordered chicken fried steak with potatoes and gravy.

Over the next hour, conversation flowed freely. Nathan was interested in everything about me, including things like where I would be going to college and why. No one had ever asked me so many detailed questions about my future, and I glowed under the interest even as I realized I didn't really know what I wanted to do with my life. It wasn't long before I told him how much I just hoped to go and live somewhere where no one knew me. Some place where I wouldn't have to be in my brother's shadow or have my parents hover over my every move. I wanted space to figure out who I was and what I desired for the long term. I also wanted discovery and adventure, and he said those were great qualities we shared.

Nathan told me that thus far he hadn't felt he could commit to a career choice because he hadn't lived enough yet to know what he wanted to do. He said he didn't intend to waste scholarship dollars when he was unsure of where he hoped to end up. I respected his explanation, feeling a hot flash of anger at my parents for judging him over his gap year when our conversation made it so clear that he was just trying to walk in wisdom and discernment. To think things through. How could anyone have a problem with that?

By the time we strolled back to the car, I really didn't want our date to end and said so. Nathan seemed to be processing that admission as we drew close to the vehicle, remaining quiet even as he opened my car door. As I shifted my body to slip inside the Camry so he could take me home, he abruptly said, "So, how 'bout it?"

"How 'bout what?" I replied, turning back to him with a smile both innocent and inviting.

"How 'bout you let me take you out again?"

I swallowed. Bit my lip. My heart was absolutely racing. "How 'bout ...," I started with a pause, "how 'bout I would like that very much?"

For several seconds we just stood there in the moonlight, our eyes locked. Then he stepped closer, putting his hand at the small of my back and gently pulling me against him. I trembled as he pushed my hair back from my face and whispered that familiar phrase once more: "How 'bout it?" This time, his voice was laced with as much passion as was about to topple me.

I arched one brow and said softly, "Well … how 'bout it?"

He leaned in to kiss me, softly and gently, and for a few glorious moments I felt myself melting. Finally, though, overwhelmed by new feelings and needing to catch my breath, I broke away and smiled in satisfaction.

"You're trouble," I announced.

Reluctantly, he let me go and we got into the car. My lips were still tingling, and I wondered whether he could say the same about his own. I was trying to work up the courage to ask him when he turned the ignition and caught me staring at him. *"You* are *beautiful,"* he said.

We didn't talk much on the way back to my house. We didn't have to. I leaned my head against his shoulder, and he rested his right hand on my left knee. I wanted to kiss more, and it made me deliciously happy to know he felt the same way.

We pulled up to my house twenty minutes early for my curfew, and he insisted on walking me to the door. I'm sure there were stars out that night, but neither of us could've seen them through the happy haze of our attraction to each other. As we stepped onto the porch, hand in hand, I held my breath in anticipation of the kind of good night parting I was sure was coming.

Just as Nathan leaned down to press his mouth to mine, though, the front door flew open.

There stood Dad, and he looked like an agitated pit bull.

2
BROKEN SPIRIT

"A broken spirit saps a person's strength."
Proverbs 17:22

"I don't want you going out with him anymore," Dad snapped after Nathan left. "He's too old for you, Jen. Besides, he's only after one thing. Once he gets it, he'll just break your heart."

That harsh prediciton ripped at the fabric of my budding romantic dreams and seemed entirely unwarranted from my perspective. I immediately rose to Nathan's defense: "You have no idea what you're talking about! He was a proper gentleman, and I had a good time."

"This isn't up for debate," Mom said, crossing her arms over her chest and standing beside my father so I'd know I was one against two. "If you see that boy again, we'll have to take your car away."

I shouldn't have been surprised by Dad's attempt to assassinate Nathan's character in my mind or by Mom's threat of grounding; after all, it was only my first official date, my parents had been sitting in our living room for hours with nothing to do but obsess, and their distrust of me and a certainty that I'd somehow turn out wrong in the end had asserted themselves often over the years. It didn't matter that I'd done things according to their own plan that night—well, perhaps with the exception of kissing Nathan on the mouth and thoroughly enjoying it.

My parents had married young and had children right off. My brother, in fact, was born when Mom was just seventeen. I'd come along unexpectedly three years later. Overall, they were good parents to us, even raising us in regular attendance at a local church. But there our pastor preached fire and brimstone every week and I'd been scared onto the straight and narrow early for fear of damnation. I knew little about, nor could I really relate to, my heavenly Father, whose love had been presented to me only in children's church and Vacation Bible School. Judgment and wrath, however, I felt I had a pretty good handle on. Such seemed to govern our home.

As my heart ached over Dad and Mom's decision regarding Nathan, I slowly went cold with the realization that they would never trust me. My good grades. Having parent-approved friendships. My careful adherence to their rules. Nothing I achieved or did mattered. They lived in fear that I'd end up as a pregnant teen, though nothing in my personal history or stated desires for my own future would've suggested it. So, after a few more heated words with them, I finally stomped to my room and shut the door with a bang. What a night it had been! I'd started falling in love for the first time and then had my heart soundly crushed by my parents within minutes.

Sniffling, I looked in the mirror over my dresser. My eyes were red-rimmed and puffy with tears, and my long brown hair was just a little messy from that wonderful kiss I'd shared. *Surely what I experienced tonight was real*, I mused. *And at any rate, isn't it my responsibility and not theirs to decide that? And how will I ever know if Nathan Nelson is 'the one' if I listen to what Mom and Dad say?* "I am going to see Nathan again," I assured my reflection. "I *will* see him."

Over the next few months, Nathan and I did continue to date each other. He just never came over to my house again. We went to the movies or to dinner whenever we had time. I'd either meet him somewhere or at a mutual friend's house. We often went out together within larger groups, too.

One day Mom almost caught me in a lie about one of our clandestine meetings. I called to check in as instructed and she said, "You're supposed to be at so-in-so's house, but I just drove by and your car isn't there. Just where are you, young lady?"

I rolled my eyes, irritated to have to be secretive about a relationship that was proving to be what I dreamed of and not at all what she and Dad expected, and explained that I'd moved on to visit another friend. I had, after all, started the afternoon where I'd said I would. I always did. Though I was technically sneaking behind my parents' backs, I really was still being a good girl. I never ditched school. I remained true to my convictions—at least in that season. And I was always home before curfew.

One saving grace in this period of tension between my parents and my choice of boyfriend was that they didn't try to stop me from talking to Nathan on the phone, something we took advantage of frequently. He would start every conversation with, "Hey there, beautiful," and I'd blush with delight. We'd talk for hours on end.

Sometime after my eighteenth birthday, Nathan invited me to go to the river with him and friends for the day. Figuring I was technically old enough even to get married without parental approval, I decided to test the waters. I asked my folks if I could join the group that would include Nathan, but my request was met with a stern no.

That refusal broke something in me. I never asked them to go out with him again. In fact, I stopped asking permission in general after that.

Thankfully, Nathan was understanding of the awkward situation in which I found myself. He was out on his own and enjoyed the full trust of his parents. And even though he could've certainly moved on to date another girl less bound by parental aggravations, he and I remained close through the remainder of my high school years—though only through e-mail once he moved to New York to pursue a modeling opportunity.

As my graduation date approached, I asked my parents to support me in going to New York University, where I hoped to lay the groundwork for a career in film. It seemed an exciting way to spend my life. Moreover, though I didn't say so, such a move would've allowed me to trail after Nathan, who'd been picked up by an agency in the Big Apple and did some bartending on the side. But, to my extreme frustration, they refused to support the idea. It didn't align with their hopes for me.

When I shared their decision with Nathan via e-mail, he immediately typed back: "Let's just run off and get married."

I nearly wept: I knew my parents would never forgive us for such a selfish move—which is how they would interpret it— and I said so. We were so young then that I felt it would be foolish to try married life without at least the possibility of their financial help should we need it.

"I'll still call you every day, Jenny," he promised.

While I believed Nathan would be willing to keep that pledge, it suddenly seemed terribly unfair of me to ask it of him. He'd already been so accommodating of every hurdle my folks had raised between us that I felt he deserved a break. So, as the tears fell, I typed: "Let's be honest with ourselves; you're an attractive and smart guy. You have your pick of beautiful women in the city. I don't expect you to keep up with me, Nathan. You are free to date who you want. I just don't want to know about it."

The reply was immediate: "None of those girls could hold a candle to you, Jen. I *will* wait for you no matter what it takes. I love you. One day I'm going to marry you."

"One day I will say yes," I replied. Then, after a promise to stay in touch, I logged off the computer, crying profusely and knowing that only God Himself could orchestrate such a thing. After all, who knew how long Nathan and I would be forced to live in different states?

In the fall of 2003, I started attending Catawba College, in Salisbury, North Carolina. It seemed like a good idea to put some physical distance between myself and my Arkansas-dwelling parents. When I enrolled, I did so with the hope of appeasing them by graduating as soon as possible and then making a break for Broadway thereafter. But my plans were frustrated by their determination to restrict my movements even from afar. On weeknights, for instance, I was to be in my room no later than eight p.m. And while I was permitted to be out until eleven p.m. on weekends, I knew that at any given midnight the dormitory phone could ring because Mom and Dad wanted to make sure that I stayed where I was supposed to be. For long months I tried to honor their requests while also finding my footing as a young adult, but I felt increasingly frustrated. And as our troublesome and contentious relationship continued to wear on me, I began to let previously held convictions slide.

Looking back, though, it is not the frustrations of trying to find my wings only to have them clipped by my parents or bent my own poor choices that most stands out as I think about my early college years. Some really good things came out of my time at Catawba.

First, I stopped going to church and started reading the Bible for myself. Simply because I wanted to. And as I did, I slowly began to gain a much richer and more accurate view of who

Jesus Christ is and why He came. It was during this time that I discovered that John 3:16, "This is how God loved the world: He gave his one and only Son, so that everyone who believes in him will not perish but have eternal life," is followed by a clarifying verse. John 3:17 says, "God sent his Son into the world *not to judge the world, but to save the world through him*" (emphasis mine). It was through reading passages like that one that I came to see that my heavenly Father, in contrast to my parents, really is for me and not against me. His rules and boundaries are like guardrails meant to help me have the best life possible; they don't change or shift with His moods or fears. Moreover, while He might allow me to face the natural consequences of a choice that ignores His guidelines, He never jerks me around like a puppet on strings. He gives me the gift of free will and allows me to use it: for my good or ill.

Second, I started opting to spend my lunch hours sitting in the cafeteria with the university's chaplain, Dr. Clapp. He was an older gentleman, always dressed in a grey suit and black tie, and something about him drew me. Soon I found myself telling him all my problems, as if he were my personal counselor. And always, without judgment and in that wonderful grandfatherly way he had, he'd answer my questions and give me biblical advice on what I should do. He spoke about God as a friend and helper, and it was after one of our conversations that I repented of my rebellious ways and decided to put my faith in Christ as Savior. And from that point forward I knew that no matter what, God would love me as His beloved daughter.

Meanwhile, Nathan and I did continue to keep in touch. And it was through one of our phone conversations that he told me his grandfather, Pop, had fallen ill with terminal lung cancer. Because that incredible man was so dearly loved and deeply influential in Nathan's life, Nathan immediately moved to

Mississippi to be with him. Nathan was his first grandson, and Pop had doted on him from birth. The pair was wonderfully close.

The relocation to Mississippi clashed with the terms of Nathan's modeling contract. So, shortly after his grandfather passed away, Nathan decided to pursue a bartending lead over in Miami. He'd heard the money was good there, and he told me that the Florida sunshine would help him heal.

Being young and having little in the way of financial resources continued to make any attempts at a distance relationship between us feel downright hopeless. So, over a long period of our being separated by hundreds of miles, even Nathan began to date other people—sometimes seriously. Nevertheless, we managed to grow closer as friends. There were even several times when the idea of getting married to each other made it into our calls and e-mails again. Nonetheless, seven long years passed between our first date and November of 2005.

After my junior year, I gave up my hopes of graduating from Catawba College or pursuing anything related to the stage or screen. Under the heavy influence of my parents, I moved to Tennessee and started living with them in their new home near Nashville. Following Nathan's example, I was bartending by the day my world took its first big shift.

I'd just arrived home from a particularly grueling night at my new job, when I threw my keys on the table and decided to call Nathan to tell him about my recent relocation. We hadn't spoken in a while, and my heart was aching to hear sympathetic words of encouragement from him. To my sorrow, though, he didn't answer his phone. And though I tried to call him the next day and the following weekend too, my voicemails received no response.

By my fourth attempt, I began to wonder whether he was intentionally dodging me—a thought that hurt. But we hadn't fought or disagreed on anything and while we spoke less often by those days and I knew he was dating a girl in Florida with some regularity, it seemed unlikely that my long-time friend would just ditch me entirely. In fact, the very thought was like a kick to my middle.

Frustrated, I stared down at the phone after I hung up and tried to keep my recently-consumed dinner from reappearing. And that's when I realized something with startling clarity. Over time, I had fallen so totally in love with Nathan Nelson, from the way he thought, to the sound of his voice, to the way he made me feel that I suddenly couldn't imagine how I'd ever let seven years pass without formally agreeing to become his wife.

I closed my eyes, allowing memories of our first kiss to overwhelm me. There was nothing I wanted more in that moment than to hold him close again.

"God, I love him so much," I prayed aloud.

And no sooner were the words out of my mouth than I knew I had to find him.

The task would not prove easy. Over the course of six months, I called every one of our mutual friends to get clues about Nathan's whereabouts. Had I known his parents' number, I would've called them even though I'd never met them. But as it was, I could only chase leads outside his family and was finally chilled to realize that no one knew what had happened to him. Even people in whom Nathan confided a great deal said things like, "It was weird, Jen. He used to call on a regular basis. Then one day he just went ghost rogue."

I'd nearly given up hope of ever finding out the truth when Nathan's old brother-outside-the-bloodlines, Colin—who'd become my friend too over the years—had an unexpected opportunity to speak with Nathan's dad. Nearly seven months had passed since his disappearance by then. It turned out that Nathan had joined the United States Air Force quite suddenly and had been in training since. Colin reported he'd chosen not to tell anyone about it lest they try to talk him out of it. No one besides his parents, in fact, had any idea he'd even been considering joining the military.

I wish I could say I felt relief at this answer to the question that so haunted my mind. But honestly, fear for Nathan rocked my heart as soon as I heard it. Back in 2001, jihadists had plowed into New York's Twin Towers and the Pentagon with passenger aircraft. Since then, America had been fighting a war against terror. Chief on the list of bad guys to take out were Iraqi president Saddam Hussein and Afghanistan's Osama Bin Laden, who had orchestrated the attacks. Reports of ongoing rocket fire against our troops in Mosul and Baghdad were discussed daily on the news, and it wasn't unusual to see on the television screen the photographs of soldiers killed in action. It was a dangerous time to be an American soldier.

Outside my basic understanding of what was going on in the world, I knew little about the military. So, as I thought about what Nathan might be up to, I kept envisioning him as either a G.I. Joe in the trenches, who faced the constant threat of an enemy suicide bomber throwing himself alongside him, or as a sniper who crouched for long months on an exposed hillside somewhere. It never crossed my mind that he'd do anything less risky.

Nevertheless, my own plans regarding Nathan had to undergo some revising. I'd admitted to myself that I absolutely wanted to be his wife if he'd still have me, but I couldn't imagine what it would be like to be married to a soldier. Such a possibility had never entered my thinking before. I was, after all, from a part of rural Arkansas that wasn't located near a huge military base and therefore had few dealings with members of the military. Jonesboro, my hometown, was full of lawyers, doctors, construction workers, factory workers, and farmers. Their children all became picturesque legacies of their parents and grandparents before them, seldom leaving the county. Didn't military families have to move around a lot? Weren't military kids labeled brats? Would a soldier even have time for a wife and children?

Such were the thoughts that flew through my mind during my bartending shift the night after Colin told me about Nathan's whereabouts. Downtown Nashville was particularly busy, and I just wanted to get back to my apartment and call it a night. I distinctly remember "Rocky Top" blaring over the band's speakers and making my head hurt.

Late into the evening, a large group of men entered the restaurant, and I sighed because I'd seen many of those clowns the night before. They were a rowdy group of soldiers on leave from Fort Campbell, which was just up the road in Clarksville, Tennessee. One of them came up to the bar and ordered a PBR Tall boy, Pabst Blue Ribbon, sliding me a five-dollar bill to pay for it and winking at me as if I was the cutest thing he'd ever seen. Though I was thankful for what I expected would become my very large two-dollar tip, I tried not to roll my eyes; this group certainly liked to throw their money around.

In fact, they were pretty full of themselves in general. The night prior, one of them had the audacity to tell me outright that I was such a wholesome little thing that I'd be perfect to take home to his mother as his wife. "But that's not what I want to do with you," he leered and then made it perfectly clear that he had no convictions regarding decency. The creep.

Thankful that my latest customer was at least the quiet sort, I turned to grab a mug for his requested drink and heard a scuffle coming from behind him. It was quickly followed by the unmistakable sound of a fist connecting with bone, a chair skidding across the floor and then against a table, and a shouted curse. As I set the customer's beer down in front of him, I saw that two of his friends were locked in a brawl. And only a few seconds passed before my manager marched into the room from the kitchen and insisted they all leave and take their chaos with them.

As I gratefully watched the group depart, I realized anew that I missed Nathan so much it hurt. He had been my person. The one young man in my life with whom I could talk about anything. He offered sound advice that wasn't judgmental or jealous or condescending. And he could never—no never—be anything like the hot-headed, fresh-mouthed soldiers my boss had just kicked to the curb.

At least, I hoped not.

3

LAST CALL

"Don't forget to show hospitality to strangers, for some who have done this have entertained angels without realizing it!"
Hebrews 13:2

Nashville's humid summer wound to a close, and though I'd just returned from a fun white-water rafting vacation with friends, I felt lonely and out of sorts. There wasn't a single day that passed that I didn't miss Nathan. My heart longed for him. Four whole years had slipped by since I'd seen him in person, and I hadn't spoken to him in months. I constantly wondered where he was and what he was doing, but I had no way of getting in touch with him. And as far as I knew, he'd done nothing to locate me. It was possible he'd even eloped with the Florida girlfriend, though I doubted it.

Down at Paradise Park, the bar where I worked, I routinely encountered other patrons from Fort Campbell. Most, thankfully, were far better mannered than the crew my boss threw out. Some of the servicemen were fresh out of boot camp, and many of them told me what it was like. They described grueling long days of physical and mental stress, being constantly yelled at by their superiors, and literally painting rocks either to pass their little downtime or just to amuse their upper cadre. Repeatedly, I heard stories about how succeeding in the military was proving to be incredibly tough.

The most haunting of these encounters happened late one night when a young soldier sat eerily quiet at the bar as my manager and I started to close shop. His head drooped down over his beer, and it seemed to me he was lost in deep thought. There were no friends around him, and it looked like he was in sore need of one, so I approached him as I cleaned glasses.

"Hey Bud," I said, keeping my tone light and kind. "We're about to close up. You good to drive, or do you want me to call someone for you?"

He looked up at me slowly, the action revealing his huge brown eyes, and answered, "No. I'm good."

Clearly he wasn't good at all, and I was concerned where his deep contemplation might lead. I told him I could see he was thinking something over intensely as he stared down at the counter, and I asked if he wanted to talk about it.

He met my gaze again. And this time I couldn't miss the sorrow lining his face: it was the only thing about him that made him look old enough to be in the service, though I knew from requesting his I.D. earlier that he was of age. He told me he was getting ready to leave on his first year-long deployment. And as if that wasn't difficult enough, his girlfriend had just broken up with him, and he didn't have the money to visit his family before he left. "I'm really scared," he admitted as tears started to fall. He quickly hung his head again to hide them, but I handed him a napkin anyway.

For just a moment, as he sat there wiping his face, my thoughts snapped to Nathan. Was he, too, afraid and alone out there in the world that night? I knew he would eventually deploy somewhere, if he hadn't already. And while I didn't know exactly what deployment would mean for him or even for the soldier in front of me, it suddenly occurred to me how awful it would be to have one's travels and physical safety tied to the government's decisions. To whatever happened on the international stage.

"Where are you going?" I asked the young solider.

He sniffled, rubbed at the remaining salty tracks on his face, and tried to sit up straighter. "Iraq."

"I'm sorry," I said. And I was.

"Yeah, thanks," he sighed. "I admit it's pretty tough not to get the chance to say goodbye in person. Things are just so uncertain, you know?"

I gave him a compassionate smile and as I continued to tidy up, he spoke about how he was going to work as a gunner on convoys. He said that was work that he liked. But in the next breath, he expressed hope that his troop wouldn't run into any IEDs, which I knew from watching the news was a reference to the bombs Taliban and Hezbollah were burying in the Middle East as part of their terrorist tactics to kill as many "infidels" as possible—particularly those who traveled in U.S. military convoys like his. The longer he spoke, the more concerned for him I grew, even as I became increasingly terrified for Nathan. I bit my lip and tried to think of what to say. It soon occurred to me that I should do for him what I'd want someone to do for me were our roles reversed.

"Mind if I pray with you before you go?" I asked just after my boss announced closing time to the near-empty room.

The customer shook his head, and—although I'd never done such a thing before—I spoke to the Lord about him right where he sat. Quietly, I asked God to calm his heart and to send His guardian angels to protect the young man and make sure he got home safely. Then, before I said "Amen," I lifted up a silent prayer for Nathan too.

When I opened my eyes, the young man was weeping. Crying his heart out like a little boy who desperately needed his Mama's hug. It absolutely broke my heart. As my boss started walking through the bar, tapping the shoulders of other lingering patrons and sternly asking them to leave, I gave the customer my e-mail address and told him I'd be happy to send him a friendly care package if he'd just send me his address. He said thanks, then my boss walked him and two other men to the door, and I watched as he slipped out into the night.

I'd never see nor hear from him again.

A few days passed in which I could neither shake my memories free of that frightened soldier nor find any rest from the ongoing urge to pray for Nathan. I hadn't been as dedicated to my new faith as I should have been in recent months—in part because I'd been so distracted by worry, so making the time to talk to God regularly again was a good change.

Another positive development happened a few nights later when I was back at the bar, shaking and pouring cocktails as a constant stream of patrons came and went. We were super busy that evening. Some people frantically waved their money in the air to catch my attention while others yelled orders at me from all directions.

About an hour into the shift, I noticed a blonde-haired girl sitting at the end of the bar. She kept eyeing me intently, as if she knew she'd seen me before and couldn't quite place me. And as I thought on it, I realized there was something vaguely familiar about her, too.

When I finally got a break from the mad rush, I walked over to her. "Hey, I know you from somewhere," I said. "What's your name?"

She smiled, tucked her short hair behind her ears, and admitted she'd been thinking the same thing about me. "I'm Ashley. What's yours?"

I told her that I went by Jena (I did by that time because I'd grown tired of hearing people pronounce the name "Jenny" the way Tom Hanks does in the movie *Forrest Gump*) and asked whether she'd ever been to Jonesboro, Arkansas.

"Sure," she replied excitedly. "I lived there when I was younger." Then she spoke of a high school she'd attended that was across town from my own.

For a couple of minutes, Ashley and I tried to decide exactly why we recognized each other but came up empty. Then, suddenly, her face lit up, and she announced that her older brother—who was only a little older than me based on my graduation year—could help us figure things out. "He knows everybody in Jonesboro," she said.

At this news, my heart started to pound strangely. I knew Nathan had a younger sister, and though I had never met her, I knew she was a blonde, and I remembered she had a name that started with the letter A. "What did you say your brother's name is?"

"It's Colin," the girl replied. "Should we give him a call?"

"Wait. What?" I laughed as she reached for her phone. "I know exactly which Colin you are talking about. I remember now! I met you at your mom's house way back, but you've cut your hair off since! There's no need to call him. Holy smokes; this is amazing! I know your brother well." Recently, I had broken my phone and thus lost the number of Nathan's best guy friend from high school. "I-I guess you'd remember Nathan Nelson, too?" I asked timidly. I just had to know if she had any insight into how to get in contact with him.

Ashley laughed delightedly, clearly eager to tell me what she knew. "Of course, I know Nate! In fact, he was just here in Nashville visiting family."

My mind was blown. For so many months I'd been worrying about the guy, and it turned out he'd been in the very city in which I lived. Maybe he'd even been in the bar at some point, and I'd just missed him.

"You want me to call Nate?" Ashley asked, flipping open her phone.

Did I want a million dollars and eternal youth? "Yes, yes I would lo—," I said, right before my manager barked my name and jabbed his thumb toward the taps so I'd remember my little impromptu break was over.

I hurried to take care of business, grateful that Ashley seemed to understand and had apparently decided to wait for me. A little later, when a couple sat down right beside her and ordered two Stella Artois, I spoke to her again as I popped their bottle tops.

By this time she'd made a new connection. "Jena's just another form of Jenny, right?"

I nodded.

Her eyes widened, and she looked like she was about to howl with excitement. "I knew it! You're the girl Nate's been going on and on about for months!"

My jaw dropped and my heart soared. What a gift it was to hear that announcement! All that time I'd been pining for Nathan, and here was evidence that he might be out there feeling the same way about me. If only I could speak to him I could find out where things really stood between us.

"Would you have a way of getting my new number to him?" I asked, quickly scribbling it across a beverage napkin.

"Girl, I'll do better than that. I'm calling him right now. When do you get clear of this place?

"Three a.m.," I smiled before hurrying off to take more orders. As I stepped up to my latest customer, I heard Ashley's strong southern voice twanging over the bar noise: "Nate Dog, you are never going to believe who I just ran into! ... I've found your Jenny!"

My middle fluttered, and I felt like I was in a dream. Starry eyed, I reached for a glass and filled it, setting it in front of the customer who'd requested a Tequila Sunrise. Ashley caught my attention as I did so and mouthed the words, "He is *totally* excited!"

I was beyond giddy myself. I couldn't believe it! At last, I had a way to get Nathan back in my life. What joy! It seemed God Himself was working out the continuation of our story—perhaps in response to all those heartfelt prayers I'd recently been sending up. I silently thanked Him, amazed all over again that He chooses to help and direct even those who feel insignificant in the grand scheme of things.

I made sure all my customers had been waited on and hurried back to Ashley. I circled a rag around the countertop in front of her to keep my manager happy while she updated me on her call. She said, "Nate's over-the-moon thrilled to talk to you! He's going into work right now, and he gets off at seven a.m. He says he'll call you after his brief. It's some kind of military meeting."

I thanked her profusely and offered to buy her and her friends a round of drinks. They happily ordered Lemon Drops, cocktails made of Vodka, lemon juice, and sugar. As I mixed and delivered them, Ashley gave me what further insight she could. She told me Nathan was living in St. Louis and routinely came to visit the Nashville branch of his family.

When she left, I marveled over the fact that I'd only met her once before—years ago at Colin's house in Jonesboro—a town nearly five hours away. I couldn't get my head around the odds of us bumping into each other in a major metropolitan city of just over half a million people, much less recognizing each other, and then making the quick and oh-so-important connections we'd made.

My cell phone sat near my register where I'd print tabs and run credit cards. For the next ninety minutes or so, I kept checking it to see if I'd received a text message from an unknown number. It was so exciting to think that Nathan was about to call! For a long time, there was nothing. But when I had less than four hours left of my shift, I found this message waiting: "How 'bout it, girl?"

Since I knew Nathan was at work, I took my time in forming a reply. Unbelievably nervous yet determined to play it cool, I finally said, "Hey there, handsome. Where have you been all my life?" I was fairly confident that those few words would convey what I needed to say without making me sound like an over-eager dork.

By the time closing approached, though, I felt vaguely disturbed that I'd not yet heard anything back. Hours had passed. Anxiety started to tighten my stomach as I counted the money in my drawer and bantered with the other bartenders.

"Did you see that drunk dressed like he was ready to play the lead character in a 'Where's Waldo?' book?" a coworker named Drew wanted to know. I nodded, and he explained that he'd had to cut him off before serving him a single drink. "Pathetic," I said. Another colleague laughed loudly at this and then told of how she'd seen a lovesick customer get up on stage around midnight, leaving the hunky guitarist with no choice but to push her off of the raised platform.

This time, I made no comment. The word "lovesick" felt pretty descriptive of how I was feeling too, though I hadn't even noticed the guitarist. Another guy owned my thoughts.

Sweet relief surged when my phone finally buzzed. "Just been missing your beautiful face," Nathan had texted. "I have to work for a few more hours. Will you be up for a while? I'll call."

It was somewhere between three and four in the morning by that time, and I was exhausted. But I wasn't about to miss the opportunity I'd been longing for. "For a bit," I replied. "I look forward to hearing your voice."

When I received a smiley face emoji in response, a million things ran through my mind. In my heart, I knew Nathan was the only guy I wanted. Would ever want. But would he find me drastically different from that girl he once knew, somehow less desirable than when we'd last spoken? Would I still find it easy to talk to him now that he'd spent months in the service? Would we still connect as we had back when we'd dated each other exclusively? And for that matter, had he set aside the Florida girlfriend, or would I find myself in competition?

I finished counting my tips and agreed to join my coworkers for breakfast, hoping their ongoing company would distract me from the butterflies fluttering in my middle. We headed to a little hole-in-the-wall diner located on First Avenue that often hosted bartenders and wait staff who'd worked the late shift and needed to socialize a little before heading home to rest up for the next night. The place reminded me of a smoke-filled Waffle House, but the hospitality there more than compensated for the lackluster atmosphere.

I ate a plateful of eggs, toast, and bacon. Then, after ninety minutes or so, we all decided to part ways. As I headed out to my car, with a coworker escorting me, I smiled to see the hot pink sunrise just cresting the horizon over the Cumberland River. It seemed like a portent that good things would happen that day—if I could manage to stay awake for them.

For a few minutes I sat in my Jeep with the doors locked, trying to decide what to do next. My phone buzzed. "Hey, Pretty," Nathan had texted. "You still awake?"

"Yeah, I'm going to go wait for the bank to open," I replied. Heading there seemed a practical way to spend my morning since I had close to eight hundred dollars on me and would soon need to pay rent.

"I'll call you as soon as I get off," he said. "STAY AWAKE!"

I headed across the city, buzzing with fresh excitement and the caffeine from the four cups of coffee I'd downed at the diner. I turned up the radio. One of the songs that Nathan and I had listened to together back in the day played: "Hey, Hey, What Can I Do" by Led Zeppelin. I smiled with the memories it brought to the surface and rolled down the windows so fresh air could blow on my face.

How well I recalled driving through rural Arkansas with Nathan on long ago summer evenings, having no real destination in mind. The whole point of those drives, in fact, was just being together. We'd talk and hold hands, and then a song like Led Zeppelin's would come on and Nathan would start to sing along loudly—as if he were standing on stage in front of seventy thousand people and letting the music take over his soul. I'd loved that he could be so free and unselfconscious. I wondered with a pang whether he would still be like that given all the recent changes in his life.

I got to the bank drive thru just as they were rolling the screens up. Mary Beth, a teller with whom I'd built some rapport, was at the window. I was on high alert, every part of me waiting for Nathan to call, and kept having to recount the massive stack of ones that I had rubber banded into piles of hundreds. Thankfully, Mary Beth was patient with me, gently correcting the number on my deposit slip without making feel foolish.

As I drove away, I realized there was nothing else to do but head toward home. I tried to think about anything other than Nathan: having dinner that afternoon with the parents across town, the laundry I needed to catch up, the hair appointment that was long overdue, the dog that needed to be groomed.

"Oh, no!" I suddenly cried as I came to a stoplight. "Barkley!" My new puppy, only months old, had been locked in my bathroom for a terribly long time. While I'd taught him to use a litter box and gated him in so that he could at least look out at the rest of the apartment, he might well have started gnawing the baseboards out of loneliness. I'd been dawdling, but my pup needed me.

I got to the Old Hickory exit to turn off to my complex and headed in the direction of the lake. I hurriedly punched in my code to open the gate, squealed into my designated parking space, and bolted out of the car and up to the second floor. The millisecond I slid the key into my lock, I could hear the yapping of my little dog. He sounded desperate.

"You poor baby," I said. "I'm coming!"

When the door opened, I got quite a surprise. Barkley rushed out to meet me, nearly knocking me over as he danced circles around my feet. Somehow he'd managed to get free of the bathroom, which meant he'd had the run of our place for who knew how long. I scooped him up, ruffling the orange fur on the Pomeranian's little wiggly body as he licked my face, and asked, "How'd you get out?" A quick glance inside revealed that the gate across the bathroom doorway stood just as I left it.

Puzzled, I put him back in the bathroom and stepped back for a minute to see whether I could get a clue about how he'd managed escape. He yapped at me, clearly frustrated that I wasn't taking him straight outside, and then disappeared to the far end of the room. Things were quiet for a second, and then I heard the rasp of his little nails on tile as he started to run hard across the floor. Then, just as he came back into view, Barkley took a flying leap at the gate. I couldn't believe it when he clung to the fencing like a raccoon on mission and walked himself right up and over the obstacle.

"Not a bad trick for a five pound dog," I laughed as he barked happily, rushed back to my feet, and begged to be picked up.

Barkley and I were outside taking care of business when my phone finally rang. I reached for it, palms damp and hands trembly.

"Hey there, pretty girl," a familiar voice said. "How the heck are you?"

To this I replied with a big smile in my voice. And just like that, Nathan and I picked up right where we'd left off some twelve months prior.

Within minutes I was pleased to hear the man I loved sounding just like his old self, though perhaps with a bit more confidence. He told me he was stationed at Scott Air Force Base in Missouri and really enjoyed it. He explained that he worked inside at a desk as an Intelligence Analyst, and not as a door kicker or fighter pilot. He also apologized that he hadn't been able to reconnect with me sooner and made sure I knew that the Florida girlfriend had long since dropped out of the picture. Everything, it seemed, had fallen into place for Nathan in the months since he'd enlisted. He'd found clarity; he'd found his calling. And, thanks to Colin's little sister Ashley, he'd found me.

"So," he said, "tell me what's happening with you."

I couldn't bring myself to reveal how I'd searched for him and worried over him for months, and I felt shy about declaring the depth of my feelings for him. So instead, I updated him on how I was living in Nashville but had been thinking about moving to Chicago for a while. Maybe looking for a job as a flight attendant. Given our frustrating history of trying to accommodate my parents, I didn't mention that part of my reasoning for considering a relocation was because they were very nearby in Ashland City, Tennessee, and still tended to be overbearing.

"You know," he said when I paused, "not a day has passed that I haven't thought about you, Jenny."

I closed my eyes, relishing that admission, and breathed deeply. The scent of goldenrod was thick in the air. How I'd missed him! And now here he was, not so very far away, sounding like he just might be as lovesick as I. But since I couldn't see his face to read his expressions and so much had happened in the months since we'd last spoken, I couldn't quite embrace his words as gospel truth.

I changed the subject: "Hey, I bet you're looking a little different these days. Don't they chop your hair off when you enlist? Just how short is it?"

"Pretty short to stay in regs."

"That's a shame! I loved your hair."

"You did?"

A long pause followed. Then he said, "Tell me what else you loved, Jenny."

My insides turned a somersault. Seconds ticked by. "Things ..."

Another silence stretched between us then, as if we were both wrestling with where the conversation should go next.

"Well," he finally said, "what about you? Do you still have long hair?"

I absently reached up and grabbed my chestnut-colored ponytail with the hand that held the leash, remembering how wonderful it felt to have Nathan's fingers running through it. "It's longer than the last time you saw me. Down to the middle of my back."

He exhaled in a rush of air. "Don't tell me you've gotten even prettier! I won't know what to do with myself."

"I will let you be the judge," I replied. "Should we get to see each other again."

"'I'll let you be the judge' is something hot girls say," he laughed, and I did too. We both knew I didn't place myself in that category.

The line went quiet for a minute. Then I heard, "So. How 'bout it?"

That was all it took to make heat instantly flood my body. Those familiar words, no matter their object, sounded so good!

"Next weekend I'll be in Nashville for my sister's wedding rehearsal," Nathan said. "Will you have dinner with me Friday?"

Play it cool, Jena, I told myself. "I have to work, but I could meet you earlier in the day."

"Maybe lunch, then, it doesn't matter."

"What about we plan for four p.m.? That's almost dinnertime, but it will still get me to work by six."

"I'll get there mid-day Friday," he said decisively. "Will leave here when I get off work and drive right down. Be thinking about where you'd like to go."

The words "anywhere with you" came to mind and I almost said them when Barkley started yipping at me, tugging at his leash to get back inside. Frustrated by the interruption, but also feeling the tug of sleep after twelve hours on my feet, I agreed to the plan and said goodbye.

The sexy way Nathan called me "Darlin'" as we hung up ensured that sweet dreams were ahead.

4

REUNITED

*"Trust in the LORD with all your heart;
do not depend on your own understanding."*
Proverbs 3:5

For me, the Friday of our big reunion began at half past one in the afternoon, a common wake time for those who work nights. I reached for my phone to silence the alarm and nearly squealed with excitement when I saw this text: "Can't wait to see you; it's been too long."

Heart singing, I threw back the covers and rushed to the bathroom sink. In less than three hours, I'd finally get to see Nathan's smile again! I brushed my teeth and washed my face, humming happily at the thought.

I changed into the outfit I'd laid out for the occasion— skinny jeans and a blouse that I could easily trade for work attire later—and hurried to apply lip gloss and mascara. Barkley, who knew not to whine to go out until I was ready for the day, parked himself at my feet and started gnawing at his favorite rawhide bone. I called it his never-ending gobstopper.

I parted my thick hair into sections and started the time-consuming task of straightening it, while thinking about the joy of the last few days. Ever since Ashley had come into the bar and reconnected us, Nathan and I had spoken daily. Not only had we talked for two hours at a time, but we'd done a lot of texting in between. It really was as if we'd picked up right where we'd left off—minus any lingering interest in dating other people at all or any mention of marriage.

For my part, I hoped the latter topic would come up again even as I feared it. I knew I'd say yes to Nathan in a blink were he to ask anew. I did, however, still feel hesitant about saying yes to the military. The more Nathan talked about how much he liked it, the better I understood what a huge part it would play in shaping his future family life. I wasn't convinced I could function in the military world.

Much more appealing was the realization that Nathan, too, had undergone some spiritual reshaping over our time apart. While I knew he'd been raised in a loving church and by parents who lived as if the Bible is true, I also knew that his boyhood profession of faith hadn't done much to mold him. While Nathan was a decent guy who generally sought to please his parents and to do most of the right things, he'd always been one who liked to fit in and to have a good time and hadn't been concerned about doing life in light of an old book's teachings. In our recent conversations, though, I'd heard him speak of attending church by choice. Of praying hard about things. Of looking to God's Word for direction. So it appeared that he, like me, was starting to slowly live out what he'd long claimed to believe. I knew my old chaplain friend, Dr. Clapp, would say such a change in both of us would make for a solid foundation on which to build a marriage.

Nathan and I had agreed to meet at Broadway Brewhouse downtown. When I got there a few minutes early for our date, I chose a seat at the far end of the bar and facing the front windows before texting to let him know I'd arrived. No sooner had I hit send, though, than did my nerves begin to tie my insides in a tangle. Suddenly I wondered what else Nathan and I could possibly find to talk about. Would I prove myself to be so socially awkward in our face-to-face meeting that he'd choose never to speak with me again?

Unreasonable panic rose, and I knew there was only one way to deal with it. "God, please calm me," I prayed.

It was almost funny when my friend Tasha suddenly showed up on the side of the counter across from me—as if she'd heard my silent request and decided to act on it. Until I sat in her shadow, her form blocking the light coming in the front of the dim room, I'd forgotten that she was the restaurant's early evening bar tender. "Hey Lady," she said with a smile on her pretty face. "You look hot! You not working tonight?"

I covertly wiped my hands against my jeans as I explained that my shift started in a couple of hours, but I was meeting an old friend for a bite to eat.

"Must be some friend! I've never seen you all dressed up like this. How long before she gets here? Is it some rich godmother you haven't seen in years?"

"No, of course not," I smiled. "It's a *he,* who will be walking through that door any minute."

Tasha grinned, having gotten the information she was obviously fishing for, and turned her head back toward the entryway. "It'll take him a minute to see you back here. I think I'll go stand closer to the entrance so I can watch for fireworks. That ok?"

"Sure," I replied.

She took two steps away from me, long curls bouncing against her back, and called over her shoulder, "What's he look like?"

I took a deep breath and released it slowly, trying to keep my voice from hitching nervously. "He's just over six feet. Athletic, slender build. Military cut dark hair. Square jaw. Blue eyes."

"Whoa," Tasha said, rushing right back to me. "You're describing an Adonis!"

I nodded, glad she knew that the coming customer was taken. "He's a good-looking man. Got a smile that will straight melt you."

She rested an elbow on the counter in front of me, leaned close, and said conspiratorially, "Glad to hear it! Thanks for deciding to come here, Jena. I could use some eye candy. I've been staring at middle aged pot-bellies for two hours." Then, with a wink, she marched out behind the counter and nearer the front, positioning herself where she could observe the coming reunion.

A few minutes later, my heart leapt into my throat when a tall, broad, shadowy figure stepped through the restaurant's open doorway. He paused just inside, turning his head this way and that as if looking for someone.

"Nathan," I breathed. Of course, he couldn't hear me. He was still too far away.

A second later, and still backlit by the outside sunshine, he stepped a little further into the shadowy room. His approaching closeness made me feel light headed. I swallowed hard, sat up straighter, and gave my hair a quick fluff, hoping to give him a pretty first impression. Though I sat nearer the back, I was more or less right in front of him. I knew that once his eyes adjusted to the lighting, he couldn't miss me.

Tasha, off toward the room's other side and behind him where Nathan wouldn't see her, waved for my attention and dramatically mouthed the words, "*Oh my!*" Then she started fanning herself as if the day and my date were so sizzling she was about to have a stroke.

Ignoring her, I whipped my gaze right back to Nathan. He removed his sunglasses, and I caught a clear view of his profile. His face looked sharper than before, matured. Gone were the long brown tresses I knew so well, short buzzed hairs on his head taking their place. He was wearing fitted jeans and a dark red Rolling Stones t-shirt that looked a little too small for his broadened shoulders, but that was certainly no reason to complain. All I could think as I watched him was that if it were so apparent to me that he'd filled out into a man over the last four years, I'd likely seem changed to him too.

I slid off the bar-height chair and stood, taking care to perfect my posture as I took a couple of steps out toward the middle of the room. That's when Nathan locked his beautiful blue eyes with mine. Had we been in a play, I'm sure the director would've cued the romantic music just then.

"Hey, stranger!" Nathan smiled, rushing up to me, and picking me up in a bear hug.

I hugged him right back, delightful dizziness nearly getting the better of me as my heart thumped against his.

"Daggum, girl," he said as he set me down and stepped back, "you look better than ever!"

I smiled at him, unable to find my tongue, as he sat down on a bar stool right beside us and motioned for me to join him.

"Wow," he said, "just wow!" And for a moment he just studied my face as if it was a priceless work of art. "I can't believe I'm sitting with Jenny." Then his voice grew softer, "My Jenny."

"Your Jenny?" I asked, raising a brow. "I belong to no one."

He chuckled at that, recognizing my teasing tone, as Tasha arrived to take our drink orders and sneak a closer look at "Adonis."

By the time she left us, I was breathing normally again and had control of my nerves. "Actually, I don't go by Jenny anymore," I said.

"Oh?"

"Yeah, *Forrest Gump's* ongoing popularity eventually ruined my name."

"The most beautiful name in the world," he said, mocking the movie while also appearing to gauge my reaction to what seemed to be his honest assessment.

"Oh, shucks, Forrest," I quoted, ducking my head in pretend embarrassment.

"Okay, then," Nathan said, "what do you prefer to be called these days?"

"Most people call me Jena. And Jennifer is fine."

He said each name aloud, as if weighing which suited me better. Then he laughed self-consciously. "I've been calling you Jenny for years—even as we've talked these last few days."

"I like it when *you* call me Jenny," I decided. "Just not in a Forrest Gump voice."

"Noted," he smiled. And for a second I thought he might lean in to kiss me on the cheek.

The moment passed, but that awkward conversation turned out to be the perfect icebreaker. Over the next hour, we ate black and bleu cheeseburgers while we stared at each other like two sappy teenagers. Tasha waited on us tactfully and customers came and went around us, but we talked careers and dreams and slowly relaxed as if we were the only pair in the restaurant.

On the whole, the visit was absolutely wonderful, but the time passed far too quickly. A wild rush of feelings linked to never wanting to lose Nathan or leave him nearly brought tears to my eyes as I glanced at the neon clock on the wall and saw that my work hour was about to start. Had I been able to afford it, I would've called in to ask for the night off.

I noted the time aloud, and Nathan called Tasha over so he could pay for our meal. As he did so, Nathan said he'd walk me down the street to work. When we retrieved my duffle bag and purse and then headed down the sidewalk, I could feel my face glowing with delight because while I would have done anything to spend more time with him, he'd been the one to suggest this clever continuation of our visit. It seemed a good sign for our future.

All too soon, though, we reached the open doorway into Paradise Park. Nathan spoke loudly to compensate for the loud country music filling Nashville's streets: "Would it bother you if I came here and hung out in a little while? I mean—after I do the rehearsal dinner?"

I smiled widely and leaned in to the hug he offered. "Of course, that's fine! It gets pretty busy here on weekends, so I may not have time to chat with you, though."

"That's ok," he said, looking deeply into my eyes. "I just want to spend time with you. No matter what."

I didn't reply to that aloud, but I gave him a look to convey that I felt the same way about him.

Over the next months, Nathan and I did a much better job of staying in touch. We spoke almost daily. Yet we still faced a huge obstacle that kept talk about a certain life-changing subject at bay. He lived four hours away in Missouri. And, as if that didn't pose enough difficulty, I had to work on the weekends when he was off and neither of us had money to spend on the flights that could only allow us a few hours together at best.

Ultimately, I decided that I might be able to improve the frustrating financial situation were I to pursue the stewardess position that I knew to be based in Chicago. Such a choice could lead into an adventurous and profitable career, and it would allow me to bank some flight time that I could use to go out and see Nathan.

I made the move, and it wasn't long before he came up to Chicago for a weekend visit. Hand in hand, we walked the Magnificent Mile and went searching for the Frank Lloyd Wright Home. Later, we even journeyed to the site of the Saint Valentine's Day Massacre and the pizza place across the street where Al Capone reportedly sat to watch those tragic events unfold. In spite of those somber stops, what I remember best about all our adventuring during those three days was that the sky was a brilliant blue and the sun shone brightly as if announcing our pleasure with one another to the whole city.

On Sunday afternoon, we were walking down Michigan Avenue, looking for a deli, when Nathan squeezed my fingers and brought up the one thing we hadn't mentioned since before he'd entered the service. "If I were to propose, what kind of ring would you want?"

"I'd like something you'd designed," I replied, having given the idea weeks of thought by that time. "Something that's just as much an expression of you as me."

"Diamond, emerald, sapphire?"

"Your pick."

I could see that Nathan was thinking hard about just what kind of setting he'd choose and was a bit overwhelmed by my suggestion, so I tugged at his arm and led him under an awning to get out of the way of all the other pedestrians. "I am *sure* I will love whatever you decide on," I said, beaming up at him.

He smiled back.

"And if I don't, then I will just say no to you."

At this, his face went stoic, and then he slowly realized I was joking. "Daggum, Jen," he laughed, grabbing his chest to indicate I'd just given him an emotional arrow to the heart. "That's a lot of pressure for a guy."

I started giggling and linked my arm in his, delighted that my biggest dream was on its way to becoming true. That I wouldn't have to figure out the future on my own anymore. "A ring is a ring, Nathan. I hope you'll be creative in picking it out, but it's you—not some piece of jewelry—I want."

We soon found the lunch stop we were hunting, but I don't remember a thing about what we ate there. The look of adoration in my man's eyes kept me too busy to notice.

Later that day, just before the sun went down and as our weekend together wound to a close, Nathan and I were walking in front of the Art Institute when a dark-haired man in suit pants, a white dress shirt, and blue windbreaker stepped into our path and held up a hand to us as if he were a crossing guard. The sight was so odd and unexpected that Nathan's grip around my waist tightened, and we exchanged a nervous glance.

When the guy drew closer, he apparently realized he was making us uncomfortable, so he bowed slightly, looked up at us apologetically, and took a large step back. When our expressions started to relax, he held up a black necktie, pointed to it and then to his own neck three times, and said to Nathan pleadingly, "Help, you me?"

The English was broken, but the man's meaning was clear. Whoever he was, he was in a hurry to someplace important and needed assistance in dealing with his unfamiliar accessory. I felt so bad for him as he threw the tie around his neck like a scarf and underscored his problem by giving the universal shrug signaling "I don't know what to do."

Nathan released me, smiled reassuringly at both of us, and gently lifted the tie from around the man's neck. He then put it around his own throat and deftly made a loose double Windsor knot before lifting the tie and situating it properly under the stranger's raised shirt collar. As Nathan made the knot snug and folded his collar down over it, a tremendous smile of gratitude lifted the man's features.

We couldn't understand a word he said as he nodded his appreciation and hurried away, but I felt like I'd witnessed something sacred. The scene provided me a unique glimpse into the gentleness and compassion that were part of my husband-to-be.

No matter what military life holds, I assured myself as we continued our stroll, *I've got a truly good man.*

5

MARRIED TO THE MILITARY

"A newly married man must not be drafted . . . or be given any other official responsibilities. He must be free to spend one year at home, bringing happiness to [his] wife."
Deuteronomy 24:5

On February 19, 2009, Nathan and I practically danced up the steps of a local courthouse to stand before a judge. I was in a dark sweater and jeans and Nathan also wore jeans, a button down shirt, and a navy pullover under his wool coat.

"You need to be really sure about this," I said as we stepped into the warmth of the building. "I'm only doing this wedding thing once. We've got to be committed regardless of what happens."

"I'm in this for life, Jenny," Nathan assured me, tugging me to his side and tucking me against his heart. "That's the way God intended it, remember?"

His words filled me with peace, bringing to mind the many conversations we'd shared since the day he asked about the ring. (He'd decided on a white-gold band with a half-carat diamond that was flanked by two smaller ones.) Nathan and I had talked at length about what we expected and wanted from marriage. We were in agreement that a married couple isn't just to share a name, roof, and bed but is to cleave together for keeps. They are to serve each other as partners and friends. Most importantly, though, we shared a deep conviction that marriage is a commitment to God. And as sure as He loves unconditionally and will never cast His kids off, a bride and groom are to remain devoted to each other in sickness and in health. Letting go only when death itself parts them.

I, Mrs. Nathan Nelson, left that courthouse feeling nervous and excited and thankful that our parents had been supportive of our decision to have a simple wedding on our own. I wasn't certain I would've had the emotional energy to deal with guests and a flood of well wishes that day because while I'd said yes to my best friend who I adored greatly, I'd also agreed to the military lifestyle, about which I still felt far less than certain. With only six weeks between our wedding day and Nathan's three-month training session out in Kansas, we needed to focus on each other.

Our honeymoon was a weekend trip to St. Petersburg, Florida. There we stayed in a modest hotel within walking distance to the beach and never thought for a moment that we should've done anything more elaborate or expensive. After all, we had one another, and that was all that mattered. Besides, Nathan vowed that we would go someplace more exciting once he returned from the upcoming deployment.

Soon I moved with Barkley into my husband's on base housing at Scott Air Force Base, outside of St. Louis. We lived in a roomy unit that had two bedrooms and a bath. The best part about our first home was that it had a fenced-in yard where Barkley could play freely. The most frustrating part was that it had to be shared with Nathan's preexisting roommate, Bill.

Bill resented my presence; after all, from his vantage point Nathan's wedding was rather sudden. And if his dislike of me wasn't alarming enough on its own, I was to share the apartment with him during the weeks that Nathan was off at training and overseas. While Nathan attempted to calm my concerns by reminding me that I didn't know another soul in Missouri and might need Bill's "safe and familiar" face should I run into car trouble while he was away, I would've preferred to take my chances. True, the roommate's presence did help us reduce costs, but I figured Barkley and I would be better off without him.

"Lord, please give me wisdom," I prayed in the apartment's bathroom after a long discussion on the Bill topic. "It looks like I'm stuck with the guy."

One answer to that prayer came through an avenue I never anticipated. Not long after I moved in, I started working at the VFW, a service organization that garners funds and support for Veterans of Foreign Wars. One Saturday I served at a VFW shootout fundraiser at which I purchased several raffle tickets. The second of those tickets won me the five-pound slab of bacon that had been donated to our cause. The next morning, when Bill found it in our shared fridge and asked about it, I offered to fry some for him. And while that move didn't exactly turn us into friends, it did lower the tension between us by a few notches.

Overall, I loved working at the VFW, where I got to visit with many widows from the World War II and Vietnam eras. The money I earned there was minimal, but the history lessons I received more than made up for it. Besides, I soon was able to secure another bartending job locally.

To fill the hours left to me so I could spend as much time away from the apartment as possible once Nathan departed, I also signed up for some business and economics classes at a local community college. I rightly figured that building such regular commitments into my life would help me to withstand the parting that was barreling down on me like a tornado making a beeline toward my bedroom.

Nathan, meanwhile, continued in his work as a senior airman at a Headquarters Air Mobility Command, or AMC. As I watched him come and go each day, it quickly became apparent that he was doing a job that truly made him happy, that challenged him intellectually. And though I'd gotten the same general sense while we were dating, there was something about daily observing his pride in his position that gave me a whole new level of respect for the path he'd chosen. So, while it might have been easier on me mentally were he to announce that after only a few short years, he'd happily transition us to civilian life, I decided to support him as he spoke of long-term plans to become a high ranking officer in the USAF and make a lifelong career out of it. Personal preferences aside, I determined that my husband would never have to shift into a lackluster job at my urging. Though I still wasn't certain what I wanted to do career wise, I made sure he felt I supported the trajectory he'd chosen.

On base, Nathan was known as The Voice of AMC because of his ability to capture an audience with his candor, personality, and overall briefing skills. This honor didn't surprise me because I'd long known Nathan to be the kind of man that could walk into any room and make friends with everyone in there before his exit.

He was so kind, masculine, and friendly that other men always wanted to know him better and women were instantly attracted to him. Soon Nathan was selected to cross over into the officer ranks as a prior enlisted member who would represent the whole community. I was incredibly proud of him. His tenacity, hard work, and knowledge had placed him in a respected position. I knew he deserved the honor.

When the time to flip our home's wall calendar page from March to April arrived, I saw that the thing I dreaded was gaining on us quickly. We'd been married less than two months, and soon we would face our first parting. Nathan had to pack up and head out to Fort Riley Military Base in Kansas, where he'd undergo a three-month training to prepare him for his first overseas deployment. And at the thought, my heart, which I'd tried to steel in preparation for the event, felt as if it had taken a bullet and tiny cracks were spreading out from it in every direction.

When the first day of training dawned, I coached myself about the importance of refusing to break down in front of Nathan. I've got to admit, though, that my determination started to slide as I watched my sweetheart sling that duffle bag over his shoulder just before he walked out our front door. It would've been less painful, in fact, had someone stabbed me. Though I'd known that the military was going to be a third party in our marriage, I fought a rising sense of rage and helplessness to see so clearly that she really did have more say than I did.

Pull it together, Girl, I told myself as I waved goodbye.

Over those weeks, every chance I got, I made the seven-hour drive from St. Louis to Fort Riley. Often I would load up the car with a backpack and a stocked cooler on Friday morning, and then Nathan and I would spend the weekend together when I got to the lodge on base. Aside from the fuel expenses, it proved an affordable way to help us cope with our first separation.

Once or twice, though, we decided to splurge on an adventure. One of my favorite date days in that period happened when we drove to Manhattan, Kansas, and visited The Wizard of Oz Museum. Hand-in-hand, Nathan and I read about the history of the movie as I marveled over my proximity to the original costumes and Dorothy's ruby slippers. After that, we found a burger joint, where we discussed how glaringly different the scarcely populated downtown area of that Manhattan was from Manhattan, New York.

Another time we decided to spend our few days together at a nice hotel. But as I started calling around to make reservations, I quickly learned that when Kansas State plays locally, all of the hotel rooms—and even the base itself—get booked up well in advance. *There's just one way to deal with this*, I decided after my fifth call. *We'll go camping.*

Hoping that May weekend would stay warmish, I borrowed a tent from a neighbor, dug out my sleeping bag, and called Nathan to tell him my plan and to ask him to get his military issued sleep cell ready. Then, after packing enough food to support our stay out in the woods, I made my way back across the grassy plains of Kansas.

What accomplishment and joy I felt when Nathan and I soon found a quiet campsite situated on a bluff and overlooking a lake! For a long time after we got out of the car, we just stood staring out over the water with our arms around each other, commenting that since we were the only ones out there, the weekend could be no less than great.

We built a cozy fire, grilled some hamburgers, and then snuggled up inside the two-person tent. How wonderful it was to hear the sounds of the wind rustling through the trees and the slow lapping of the water hitting the rocks below our bluff as we looked up through the mesh screen of our roof to watch stars slowly appear. Contentment made me sleepy, and I eventually nodded off in my husband's arms.

Within what seemed like only minutes, though, I heard Nathan anxiously say, "Jennifer, wake up!" He kissed my forehead and gently nudged my shoulder before repeating himself more sternly.

I blinked up at his shadowed face for a moment, surprised when a big, cold raindrop landed right on the tip of my nose. I hurriedly sat up too, immediately aware that the air had changed while we slept. It was freezing outside, and everything inside the tent was soaking wet.

"It dropped into the thirties," he commented, pressing additional clothing into my arms as he scrambled outside to close the rain flap and stir the fire.

As I pulled a half-soggy sweatshirt over my head, I could see the glow of his flashlight and heard him poking around in the woodpile. A minute later, he leaned inside to report that the fire was out and the rain had drenched our wood supply. "Come on, babe," he said, passing me my shoes that were sitting in the doorway. "Looks like we'll be spending the rest of this night in the car."

Wordlessly, I followed him back to the vehicle and got in. Nathan turned the ignition and we sat there for a few moments, shivering, before he could turn the heat on full blast. Even that wasn't enough to cut the chill of sitting there in skimpy wet garments, though, and Nathan announced what I'd started to suspect: "We need to head over to Walmart. Without some dry clothing, we might not last the night."

That particular visit to Kansas will live on forever in my memory, mostly because I was so upset that I'd failed at creating what was supposed to be a romantic campout. But the next visit, my last one to meet Nathan at Fort Riley, lives on in my mind for a different reason.

By that weekend, the specter of what else lay ahead of us refused to be ignored. Only hours stood between us and his first overseas assignment. And as we lay in our hotel bed, our limbs intertwined as we discussed our pending parting, my heart squeezed. I tried to hide my tears in the blanket that I'd positioned between Nathan's muscular bare shoulder and my face, but I was sure he knew about them. I'd never felt more afraid, never more sad.

Nathan usually did a much better job of remaining stoic in emotional moments than I did, but he too had a few tears escaping that night. And though he looked away from me and tried to discard them covertly, he wasn't fooling anyone either.

"I'm not scared of dying, Jenny," he finally said as he gently combed the ends of my hair with his fingertips. "Thanks to Jesus, I know where I'm going if I do. But I am afraid of leaving you behind. I hate that thought."

"Why's that?" I sniffed, reaching up to brush trailing wetness from his stubbled cheek. I sensed that he needed to talk the matter out.

"I-I'm afraid of becoming so badly injured or disfigured that you'd have to take care of me. I don't want that for you."

Fierce love for him made me hug him even closer. "I will do *anything* for you, Nathan. Remember? I made you and God a promise. If something happens, I *will* do whatever it takes."

"But I don't want to be reliant on you, Jen. I don't want to be a burden."

I scooted back a bit and propped my head on my hand so that I could look him right in the eyes. "What if something happened to me, Nathan? Wouldn't you be there for me?"

"You know it!"

"Yes, I do know. I know that wholeheartedly. Nathan, honey, we've both promised a thousand times to do whatever it

63

takes just to have more days together. To make up for all those years we had to be apart. So, let's try not to think about all this anymore, ok? Let's trust that it will work out. That God will provide."

He wiped his face with the heel of his hand and said, "I love you so much."

"And I love you, too," I assured him with a long kiss.

The next morning as I dressed, I wanted to throw up. My best friend was about to board a plane and embark on a journey that would take him out to war torn Afghanistan, and I knew plenty of soldiers had left for that area only to return in caskets or with debilitating injuries. Just as troubling, though, was the fact that many of the latter had been met stateside by spouses who'd chosen to walk away rather than stand by them. As I watched my handsome best friend lacing up his boots, I asked God to help me prove to be made of stronger stuff than they should the need arise.

We had only been married three and a half months that June when Nathan and I drove to the airport to say goodbye. Only two weeks of that time had been shared under our roof. Wishing for more, I clung to my husband's hand the whole way there, too full of roaring emotions to speak.

Upon arriving in the airport's garage, Nathan parked the car, turned off the old Dodge Intrepid, and shifted in his seat to face me. Then he reached for my free hand so that all our fingers were intertwined, his blue eyes solemn. He bowed his head, and I followed his lead as he prayed aloud: "Dear heavenly Father, we come to You today to ask that You watch over us. We know that You are the Master over all things, and we want Your will to be done in our lives. Whatever it is. I ask that You give Jenny strength and peace while I am away. May she be comforted by Your presence. In Jesus' name I ask it. Amen."

Then I verbalized my own requests for Nathan: "God, I ask that You surround my husband and his unit with legions of protective angels. May they stand guard around them during their time in country. I ask that You bring Nathan home with all ten fingers, all ten toes, and his sanity. It's for this I pray, in Jesus' name. Amen."

After that, with our faces wet and hands trembling, Nathan and I sat for a moment and just stared at each other. I silently asked God to help me find my voice again before I said, "We'll be okay, Nathan. Just got to put on the full armor of God, right?"

He nodded, well familiar with my reference to Ephesians 6:10-18. "Be strong in the Lord," he quoted, "and in his mighty power. ... Resist the enemy in the time of evil. Then after the battle you will still be standing firm. ... Put on salvation as your helmet, and take the sword of the Spirit, which is the word of God."

"And pray in the Spirit," I finished. "At all times and on every occasion. Stay alert and be persistent in your prayers."

"I will," he said solemnly.

"And I will, too," I said.

Knowing there was nothing more to be discussed, I wiped a tear from Nathan's cheek and then another from my own.

A certain measure of peace claimed my heart as we got out of the car. It still hurt dreadfully to know I had to say goodbye, but the prayers had helped me remember another Bible verse that seemed particularly appropriate and bracing. Joshua 1:9 says, "Be ... courageous! Do not be afraid or discouraged. For the LORD your God is with you wherever you go." Indeed, neither of us had to face the frightening future alone.

We made our way to ticketing, where I was given a pass to walk with Nathan up to the gate. I may have imagined it, but it seemed like the airline desk attendant gave me a look of sympathy as she handed it to us.

When we turned from our conversation with her, I allowed myself to look around. Surrounding us was a huge number of camo-clad soldiers, each one bearing a rucksack and footlocker. It was an overwhelming sight in that tiny airport. And it was made even more intense because so many of those soldiers were accompanied not just by spouses but by teary-eyed children clinging to their legs or hands.

Every step Nathan and I took through that crowd made my heart thud painfully as my mind raced. For a few panicked moments, I entertained the ridiculous idea of borrowing one of the airport security carts that zipped past us so I could kidnap Nathan and force him into hiding. I wish I could say I dismissed that temptation easily. But the only real deterrent was knowing that if a solider goes AWOL, that is, absent without leave, he'll eventually be caught and jailed.

By the time we reached the gate, I found that there was a lump the size of a prize-winning watermelon in my throat. My husband, my friend, my Nathan stood before me, painfully handsome in his Airmen Battle Uniform as his gear rested at his feet. The bold-faced word NELSON was taped to the back of his combat backpack, mocking my grief with a glaring reminder that partings like this one were to be my lot in life. That thought did nothing to make things easier.

"I love you so much," I said, lifting up on my toes to give him a thorough hug and kiss.

"I love you, too," he said, his voice thick.

The airline attendant announced that boarding was beginning, and I stepped back and refused to allow myself to wail like I wanted. Nathan touched my cheek affectionately, and I managed a wobbly smile. "See you at Christmas," I said.

He nodded, picked up his pack, and followed orders like the good solider that he was.

Just before I lost sight of him in the gathering crowd of passengers, I remembered our haunting conversation of the night before. *Does he really question whether he'll come home intact?* I wondered. And then I decided I didn't want to know.

Besides, as an intelligence analyst for the 82nd Airborne, Nathan likely wouldn't march directly into harm's way over there. Much of the time he'd work at a desk, searching through documents and resources to see what intel should be passed along to the leadership to help supplement the army's intelligence offerings. Through briefings, he'd alert them to new threats to ground or air operations, any pertinent shifts in international politics, or the rise of different world conflicts that might impact the fight. All of this would be done within a SCIF, a Sensitive Compartmentalized Information Facility, which was essentially an office space with heavy security. "I'm not a door kicker," he'd assured me a dozen times.

As the days of our separation stretched into months, I struggled to adjust back to solo life. There was plenty to do. I had my college classes, and I'd started taking extra shifts at work because busyness is one of my most effective distractions. There were also the usual home jobs to cover, things like grocery shopping, dish washing, and keeping up with the laundry. (Not to mention cleaning Bill's hair and shaving cream residue out of the shared bathroom sink.) And I had extra financial responsibilities in that I had to keep up with my own payments as well as the ones Nathan typically covered. Moreover, when his car's front end started making a thudding noise, I had to figure out how to address the eleven-hundred-dollar pinion repair.

I called Nathan's dad, Tom, for help as it dawned on me that I was facing just the kind of expensive emergency situation that Nathan had feared. (It turned out Bill wasn't as much assistance with handling car trouble as he'd hoped.) I was both surprised and deeply touched when my father-in-law insisted on paying the massive bill himself and encouraged me to start looking for a new car. "No need to drop another dollar into that worthless hole," he chuckled. "I knew that Dodge wouldn't last long when he bought it. Will you please let me help purchase another one for you two?"

Though I was deeply touched by the generous offer, I feared it was too much and almost argued. Only when I remembered how Nathan had talked about his father's open-handed ways and how I should always be willing to let him aid us if we needed it did I gratefully agreed to Tom's proposal. Even so, I researched for weeks to find a pre-owned vehicle that would prove reliable as well as affordable for him. Eventually I settled on a Jeep Patriot that had only thirty thousand miles on it. By the time the Dodge trade-in and Nathan's military discount were deducted from the invoice, I felt I'd made a wise choice that Tom could feel good about supporting.

With so much going on in that season, the days started to pass quickly. But the long, lonesome nighttime hours remained the worst. Hating to cook dinner for one and not willing to make a habit of cooking for Bill, I routinely ate budget-friendly microwave meals, often Lean Cuisines, curled up with Barkley beside me, and tuned my bedroom's television to a station that played documentaries. Many times the droning sound of narration lulled me to sleep.

Initially, I'd tried to make other friends and break things up by attending evening squadron spouse events on base. But as a first-year military wife who was yet to understand all the ranks and acronyms that were such integral parts of their lives, I felt awkward among them. For a while, though, I told myself that seeking their company was important and pushed through my hesitations. But one night, at a potluck, I stood in a small circle of wives who looked to be ten years or so older than me. We'd been making small talk for a few minutes when I made the mistake of admitting how much I was missing Nathan, how deployment was proving to be even tougher than I'd expected.

"So this is only your first time apart?" a woman with frizzy, graying hair asked, her voice cold and her face—shockingly—amused.

I nodded, feeling uncomfortable. The other wives around us seemed to be staring at me, and I suddenly was certain that the three months of training I had weathered weren't worth mentioning.

The gray-haired woman's tone was sharp as she lifted her chin and said, "I'm on deployment number nine, honey. And I did them all while taking care of four kids. Talk to me about your problems when you know what that's like."

Mouth ajar and eyes wide, I gathered the shreds of my dignity and then politely excused myself from the gathering. After that, I long stayed away from such things.

One of the few bright spots in my life during this period can be summarized in five words: the miracle of communication technology. Nathan and I e-mailed one another as often as we could, and we were even able to speak for a few minutes each day—at least most of the time. I can't adequately explain what a wonderful relief it was to hear him start each call with a joyful, "How 'bout it, woman?"

One evening in mid-August, he called me from Afghanistan just before his breakfast hour. As I reached for my phone, I was delighted to see that this would be a FaceTime call, essentially a videoconference. His smiling countenance on my screen was the best thing I'd seen in weeks.

We spoke about how he'd unexpectedly run into a cousin in the lunch building, how the two had caught up over rice and chicken. Then, just as I started to tell him about my day at school, my words were interrupted by a terrible, whistling scream.

It raised the hairs on my arms.

Chest pounding as if I'd just run ten miles on a hot day, I realized that what I'd heard was coming from Nathan's danger-filled desert world. And with horror, I watched as my husband's eyes grew wide and he quickly looked up. I wanted to ask him what was happening, but before I could say anything at all, the image on my screen froze and the call dropped.

For a second, I stared down at the dark screen in disbelief. Then I started to shake. And though I frantically tried to reconnect our chat for the better part of an hour, my fears were left to grow.

Finally, cold with shock, I did the one thing I knew stateside military wives are never supposed to do. I turned on the news.

6
DUTY CALLS

"Be on guard; stand firm in the faith."
1 Corinthians 16:13

As I used the remote to flip back and forth between each of the major news stations, I paced a trail into the bedroom carpet. Updates on celebrities, discussion about some issue up for a vote in Washington DC, and a story about how a man was trying to set a world record taunted me. Would those perfectly polished network anchors never get around to discussing the rocket attack in Afghanistan that I'd just witnessed? *Or*, I wondered feverishly, *could it be that they don't know about it?* Maybe the whole thing was so much bigger and scarier than I could guess that the government had chosen to suppress the matter.

One hour without any information on what I'd heard passed into two. And though I'd mentally braced myself to see a car pulling up to the house so that some uniform-clad higher-ups could deliver condolences, nothing happened. It was like waiting forever for an oncologist to confirm that what you've self-diagnosed as advanced cancer really is past treatment. But even worse was the ongoing silence from my phone.

Just as I was about to go mad with worry, I came across a wonderful message waiting in my e-mail box: "Hey, babe, sorry about that. A mortar round hit the base and knocked out the Internet. I went for breakfast and am sitting in the office. Get some rest. I'll try to call tomorrow. Love you, hubby."

After reading that, I let out a huge sigh and dropped into the chair that faced my computer. Anxiety slowly hissed out of my body like air escaping from a deflating balloon. I closed my eyes, propped my elbows up on the desk, and put my head in my hands, feeling listless and totally spent. I was certain that when next I looked into a mirror, I'd see white strands in my hair and a few wrinkles marring my complexion. The colossal amount of panic that had just coursed through my body had worked on me like an electric shock. I wasn't sure I'd ever recover.

Barkley helped to right my emotional world when he jumped up into my lap and wiggled his way between my arms, licking my face to offer whatever comfort he could. Smiling absently, I scratched behind his pointed ears and kissed his head. Then I rose and took him out on his leash, drawing in some fresh air and trying to focus on the gusts of wind that graced my bare arms and the dull hum of jet engines as they passed above— anything to help me move past the scare.

After we'd walked the perimeter of our patch of grass three times, I looked down at my dog and asked, "I need a hobby to take my mind off things, don't I, Bud?" Then we returned inside and went to bed until it was time for me to dress for work.

Thankfully, the remaining two months of deployment one passed without incident.

Just before Christmas, the day of Nathan's return dawned. I spent over an hour on my hair and makeup, working to look my best. I pulled his favorite dress, a sassy red Calvin Klein number, out of the closet and over my head and stepped into a pair of strappy nude wedges. Though I didn't realize it at the time, I was starting a welcome-home-Nathan tradition. Given all that he'd surely seen and had to endure during our time apart, I wanted to make sure he felt welcome. To help him know that all that wartime ugliness was behind him.

Operational Security had sent me a five-hour window of possible landing times for my husband's plane and absolutely no flight documentation. Thus, I found myself sitting in the airport's baggage claim area for half a day, surrounded by hurried travelers and exposed to constant blasts of winter air as those who'd gathered their bags rushed past me to catch taxis and shuttles outside. Since I was alone and couldn't talk to Nathan because he was in the air somewhere, I passed the time by allowing my mind to wander.

On one hand, I felt very proud of myself. I'd made it through six whole months without my husband's comforting presence and had that awful, dreaded first deployment behind me. Further, I knew Nathan would be pleased to see that our place was clean, that our closet looked tidy, and that our savings account was bigger than when he left. Moreover, I'd be able to report that I had bothered the squadron only once in his absence: I'd needed help unloading a thrift store chair for the living room. (Bill was seldom around when I actually needed him.)

On the other hand, I struggled with a nagging fear where Nathan was concerned. He'd been nothing but his kind and supportive self during our many communications. But lately I'd heard stories about PTSD, Post Traumatic Stress Disorder. Just knowing that such a thing existed was jarring enough, but one of the wives had recently shared about how her husband returned from his first overseas assignment as a new, and much crueler, man. "He woke me up out of a sound sleep," she said, her chin quivering at the memory. "His hands were around my throat, and I honestly thought he was going to kill me, Jennifer. In his mind, I was one of *them*." Since Nathan and I had only lived under the same roof for two weeks of the last nine months and he'd never shipped off to a combat zone before, I was keenly aware that I really couldn't know what to expect.

"Please, God," I begged, "help him be the man I remember."

Minutes later I forgot my fears when I caught my first glimpse of Nathan, who was strolling in my general direction. I stood up, hurriedly shed my bulky coat, and smiled timidly, desire for my man quickly rising as I realized that he'd gained at least twenty pounds of muscle while down range.

"Jenny!" Nathan laughed when he saw me, his booted feet quickly closing the remaining distance between us. He picked me up by the waist, spun me in a circle, and gave me a kiss that made my head swim. The reunion was so marvelous that by the time we got home, I was mentally assuring myself that nothing bad could ever happen to us.

Indeed, the next few weeks were nothing short of perfection. We spent a lot of time in bed, making up for lost opportunities. And slowly we relaxed into the kind of married life normalcy we'd previously been denied. Nathan went to work in the evenings, and I worked and took classes by day while he slept. Though it may seem that such schedules wouldn't leave us much time for one another, things felt luxurious compared to the way they'd been. We were able to eat dinner together consistently—

usually without Bill—and I got the privilege of packing six peanut butter and jelly sandwiches and the previous night's leftovers into Nathan's lunch cooler each morning. Things were fantastically normal, even humdrum at times.

In retrospect, as I try to pinpoint what went so horribly wrong after those glorious days right after that first big homecoming, I'd have to say that my husband and I started to fall into the temptation to worship one another rather than God.

That might sound extreme, but I remember one Sunday morning when the first thing I saw upon waking up was my sadly dust-covered Bible sitting on the nightstand. I hadn't opened it in months, even though I had been praying for God's protection consistently all throughout the deployment and truly believed that He was responsible for bringing Nathan home safely as asked. Worse, since Nathan's return, most of our Sunday mornings had been spent under the sheets with our bare bodies intertwined. While I honestly loved the way things were going and knew married sex to be God's invention and that He is pleased when people enjoy His good gifts, I recognized it was wrong to elevate its importance over Him. Our lazy days of passion for one another really were replacing devotion to the God we claimed to serve.

Importantly, the concern really began to nag me later that week when I realized that while Nathan and I had no problems communicating in our room, we were slowly losing touch with each other outside it. Gone were the hours-long chats we'd once shared. Little was said about feelings or personal needs or expectations. In fact, we rarely spoke more than a handful of words to each other over dinner or in passing. The situation reached a tipping point one evening when I got home and Nathan gathered his things for work and didn't even say goodbye before he headed out the door. I was so hurt by that choice. What I'd thought was the tightly woven cloth of our marriage abruptly seemed to be fraying at the edges.

Devastated, I went to a friend with my concerns.

A long-time military wife herself, she didn't seem a bit surprised by what I shared. And, ominously, she gave this warning: "Soldiers feel more like themselves when they're not home, dear. Don't be surprised when he volunteers to deploy more frequently."

Looking back, I suspect that it was my obsession with that disturbing comment that started the big fight.

That very afternoon, Nathan mentioned in passing that he wanted to spend that night, Friday evening, with the boys.

"Seriously? With *them*? You know I don't trust these guys, Nathan," I snapped.

"Just for a couple of hours, Jenny."

"But they are constantly trying to put you down to make themselves look better! Why, just last week, you told me—"

"It's just the way of our work relationship, Jennifer. You're too hard on them. Besides, I could use some guy time away from work. You can understand that, right?"

"What I understand," I said loudly, "is that you've been listening to Bill go on and on about how I, in marrying you, stole his Wingman. And now here you are telling me that you are planning a date night—not with me—but with him and the guys after being gone six whole months!"

At this, Nathan retorted that I was being controlling, a charge against which I loudly defended myself. But then, rather than arguing back or offering to adjust his plans so we wouldn't lose the whole evening together, he did the unpardonable. "I'll be back later," he said. Then he headed out the door and got in the car, where Bill was already sitting. And just like that, the two of them drove away to do the thing I'd not wanted Nathan to do.

Frankly, that completely enraged me. Poor Barkley had to listen to my subsequent venting and watch my frenzied pacing, and he finally hid himself under the couch to escape.

Somehow, seeing him under there, those big, innocent eyes turned up at me in puzzlement and even a little fear finally calmed me. "I'm sorry," I told him, offering a dog biscuit and sitting on the floor beside him to let him know the storm had passed.

Timidly, he reached for the treat.

"I'll give Nathan time to cool off," I told the dog. "Then I'll call, apologize, and we'll work on putting this whole thing behind us."

But several hours later, when I tried to phone my husband, he declined the call. And worse, he didn't come home even as daylight approached! I was absolutely crushed by that choice because while it was uncharacteristic of Nathan, it was just the kind of thing I would expect one of his friends—and especially Bill—to suggest he do.

Angrily, and with eyes and nose running, I spent the early hours of the morning packing all of my things into suitcases. And when my husband finally did show up, my overflowing bags by the kitchen table were the first thing he saw.

"So you're leaving me, Jenny?" Nathan said as Bill dodged us and went on back to his bedroom. "Just like that?" Were I not so completely drained, I might have tripped our irritating roommate as he sauntered by. He had the gall to snicker at our quarrel as he passed.

"If you want to talk, sit down," I said to my husband.

"I want to go to bed," Nathan quipped as he lowered himself beside me. "I'm tired."

Still seething, but trying to sound calm, I didn't mention that I hadn't slept all night either. I simply replied, "I hope your adventurous night away was worth it."

He looked at me blankly and then glanced uncomfortably at my luggage again. "So this is it? I don't get a second chance?"

I stood up. "Look, I'm not going to ask you what you did all night or even where you were. I don't have to because I know who you were with, and I know what that group does in its off time. Bill is a creature of habit, and to date, I've lived under a roof with him even longer than I've lived with you. So I'm telling you right now, husband, that I deserve better than to be left behind here while you bar hop."

To his credit, Nathan looked repentant.

"Last night you left your life partner behind," I said, hoping the language would resonate with my soldier. "You get one and only one of those mistakes as far as I'm concerned. I have committed to you, given up a lot for you, and managed your affairs stateside while you were gone. I know how to take care of myself. So, know this. While I don't need you, Nathan Nelson, I want you. And I was serious when I made our marriage commitment. I deserve to know that you can say the same. You owe me that."

Before that morning was done, I unpacked my bags, and Nathan and I fell into an uneasy truce. But three weeks later, and less than three months since his return from Afghanistan, Nathan left again—this time for another two-week training.

During the first three days of that separation, I went out to eat with a few friends I'd met on base. I well remember that the mood of the meeting was depressing, as if none of us could find anything positive to say about anything. Over appetizers, we commiserated over our separate frustrations with life and all the ways that real-life marriage fails to align with storybook expectations of it. "Nobody tells you about all the financial struggles," one friend grumped. "Or how hard it is to hold Prince Charming's attention," another sniffed; her husband of five years had a girlfriend on the side. "And I certainly wasn't warned about being screamed awake," added a woman whose partner had suffered from terrible night terrors since his second deployment. All in all, it was one of the most discouraging hours I'd ever spent.

The good news is that by the time I got home, it was as if a fog had lifted. Between the restaurant and my front door, I'd resolved that while I couldn't change the frustrations that went along with Nathan's job, things in me needed immediate correction. In fact, were I to avoid becoming an embittered old shrew, I absolutely needed to get back on track with my faith. Previously, seeking God though reading Scripture and spending time among other believers had offered me peace. Direction. Hope. I had every reason to believe they would do the same again if I'd just give them a chance.

Feeling lighter at the thought, I dusted off my Bible that night and turned to 1 Corinthians 13:4-7, a familiar passage that I suspected would speak right to my tired heart. I read it aloud, considering each phrase both in terms of how I could love my imperfect husband better and as a reminder of how very much and how very well God loved both of us in spite of the way we'd been neglecting Him: "Love is patient and kind. Love ... does not demand its own way. It is not irritable, and it keeps no record of being wronged. ... Love never gives up, never loses faith, is always hopeful, and endures through every circumstance."

7
MOVING AND GROWING

*"After you have suffered a little while, [God] will restore, support,
and strengthen you, and he will place you on a firm foundation."*
1 Peter 5:10

Over a year had passed since I decided to recommit our
marriage to the Lord, and within those months came many
changes. While Nathan hadn't deployed since 2009, things were
rarely static for us. For instance, over a twelve-week period, I
stayed with family in Tennessee while he attended officer training
at Maxwell Air Force Base down in Alabama. (How odd it was to
move back in with the folks during that season, again working
behind my old bar at Paradise Park.) Those frustrating weeks
turned out to be worthwhile, though, when Nathan graduated as a
butter bar lieutenant. I was so proud of him as we reunited over
commencement weekend.

Yet even more important than his career advancement was
the way he chose to reprioritize the Lord's position in his life and
our marriage, too. Slowly, and often timidly at first, he began
talking to me more about faith's importance and how he really
didn't want to do life without it. When he was home, he started
seeing to it that we always prayed together at dinnertime and

before bed. He'd take my hand and speak to the Lord about how much he loved me, telling Him how thankful he was that He'd led us to one another. And as things like this become increasingly normal for us, our dedication to one another deepened. Rather than just turning to one another for pleasure or for security, we began to treat one another as valued partners. To make romance, and not just its climax, a regular part of life. We were cleaving together, just as we'd long dreamed a couple should.

After Nathan's graduation, we moved to west Texas where he could finish eleven more months of schooling. It was during that time that Nathan and I first started working to surround ourselves with Christian friends who could help us grow in the faith. And it was also there that Nathan bought me my first gun and, each Sunday after church, taught me how to shoot it. He saw such training as part of the job of loving and protecting me well. I saw it as a fun way to spend afternoons with my man.

In Texas, things were good. There we found a comfortable normal that didn't include Bill or our parents. We even routinely hosted casual potluck dinner parties and played cards with shared friends. But just as I started to envision that peaceful state lasting, Nathan and I received new orders.

They came when we were on base for an official drop ceremony. Nathan in his ABUs and I in fitted jeans, boots, and a cream-colored blouse, entered the hall full of airmen waiting on their assignments from officer intel school. When the name Lieutenant Nelson was called, Nathan and I were given a red balloon with our last name on it. We knew the orders were on a slip of paper hidden inside.

Nathan handed me a pin and held the balloon steady as I prepared to pop it. Though I wasn't thrilled with the idea of moving again, I'd known it was inevitable and had determined to join my husband in his excitement over the change. So, as I drew back my arm and aimed for the center of the red orb, we were both grinning like kids set to spend the day at Disneyworld. We couldn't have been more anxious had we been on the cusp of a gender reveal.

With a loud snap, the balloon exploded and a white piece of paper fluttered toward our feet. Nathan grabbed for it. "Mildenhall, United Kingdom!" he read aloud as the crowd around us cheered.

"England!" I shouted, genuinely pleased about the news.

That next day I began charting a course for our move. I started a three-ring binder in which to keep notes on things like housing options near our new base, how to get Barkley there according to international rules, and what the relocation timeframe would look like. I was making real progress when all my planning hit a boulder.

Nathan came home early one afternoon and found me in the office. Pleased to see him at that unexpected point in the day, I immediately launched into news of the latest exciting aspects of my UK research. But when I saw the somber look on his face, I stopped. "What's wrong?" I asked.

"New orders," he said. "We've been re-routed, Jenny. We aren't going to England after all."

"Not going?" I asked, trying not to sound as disappointed as I felt. "But, but I made plans."

"I'm sorry," he said. "We'll have to change them. I'm needed at Joint Base Lewis-McChord."

"Where's that?

"Tacoma. Washington state. Looks like a four-year assignment."

"Wa-wa-washington state?" I asked, hating how wobbly and tearful it had come out.

He studied my face, looking concerned.

At the sight of compassion in his beautiful blue eyes, I couldn't help myself. I stood up, threw myself into his arms, and began to sob. How in the world would I ever survive a move to the Pacific Northwest? It lacked all of the glamor I associated with the move to the land of the royal family and endless sightseeing opportunities. Worse, all I knew about it was that it had a reputation for being a dreary, rainy, and otherwise depressing place. I was certain I'd be unable to live there for the years assigned to us—particularly if that meant further trainings and deployments that would deprive me of my best friend for months at a time. Worse, such relocation would cut me off from all other friends since I reasoned that no one would be willing to travel out that way.

"Let's sit down," Nathan said, maneuvering himself into the desk chair and pulling me into his lap. He kissed my temple as I leaned into the embrace. "It's going to be okay, Jenny. You'll find a job, make new friends. You'll adapt. Overcome."

I knew he was right, but I didn't have to like it and told him so. I also made sure he heard my list of fears and anxieties, which he accepted with so many nods and comforting caresses that I realized it would be selfish of me to say more. Determined to change my tone, I sat up straight and wiped my eyes. I'd been around the military long enough to realize that being a good solider is a choice. "Well, crumb! I was really looking forward to that UK assignment," I said with a sniff and an encouraging smile. "Tell me what you know about Tacoma."

Nathan's face lit up at the sudden display of interest; he was no doubt relieved that I'd decided not to brood. I could see that he was amped up about what lay ahead. "Actually, it's an *amazing* opportunity. I'm assigned to the 22nd Special Tactics Squadron. Will be working with the Special Tactics guys."

"What's so special about 'em?"

"Well, you've heard of Green Berets in the army, right?"

I nodded.

"The Special Tactics guys are Red Berets for the Air Force. Think of them as combined teams of special operators. They jump out of air craft, set up air strips, and ..."

For several minutes, he spoke animatedly on the subject, making my head spin.

"Babe," I finally said, "can you speak civilian? I don't know what any of that means." By that point, I was envisioning Nathan jumping out of a plane with guys in red berets and free-falling into a desert zone. For all I knew, he'd fire a flamethrower at bad guys from the back of a motorcycle next.

Nathan chuckled at the expression on my face and reiterated that he'd just been handed a fantastic opportunity, way better than the Mildenhall assignment. Then he went back over what he'd just said, substituting real words and laymen's terms in place of the string of acronyms and specialized language used previously.

"Good grief." I giggled to release some of the tension I felt. "Is that what you were trying to tell me? It's much less scary that way."

He laughed along with me as I stood up and moved toward the kitchen to figure out what to make for dinner.

"You know," I said over my shoulder, "Uncle Sam really ought to present every family in service with a copy of *Military Language for the Civilian*. It's awful hard to follow all that stuff when it isn't a part of the way a person speaks on a regular basis."

He agreed and announced he'd better get started packing.

"Wait, what?" I asked, coming to a halt. "When do we have to report?"

"End of the month," he said, not missing a beat.

I spun on my heel to face him. "But I can't be ready that fast! I have to throw out the Europe binder and start a new one. And then there's the fact that I'm sure it will take us a week to get out to Washington. That's not something I can plan in a few days."

"We *can* do it," he assured me, pulling me close again and giving me a quick kiss. As he stared down at me with excitement in his expression, I knew I'd have to be on board with making it happen.

As suspected, moving day came very quickly. Nathan, Barkley, and I headed out to Tacoma in a box truck that would serve both as transport and sleeping quarters throughout our five-day journey. To break the monotony, I decided to create a playlist of every song I could think of as we traveled. It included everything from Hank Williams Senior to Led Zeppelin. Working on the collection did help to pass the time, and we sang along with the changing genres of music as the miles separating America's western south from its north shortened.

About the time we crossed into New Mexico, I started to use my phone for house hunting outside the new base. That led me to an interesting article about the Puget Sound area, which immediately set my imagination spinning. But though I tried to talk Nathan into just renting a houseboat within that beautiful inlet rather than buying a house as he'd determined to do, he wasn't interested.

"But, Babe, just think of it," I said. "Imagine coming home at the end of a hard day and hearing the sound of waves gently lulling you to sleep!"

"How 'bout I'll pass?" he laughed. "Besides, you know I'm hoping to set up a wood shop out here. I won't have a place to work in if my backyard is the Pacific."

My suggestion that we do some sightseeing en route met better success. We stopped in Albuquerque and Roswell, New Mexico, took pictures at the edge of the Grand Canyon, and marveled at the Petrified Forest and Painted Desert. We also went to see the Avenue of the Giants in Humboldt County, California. But where we parked the truck on the night of that visit is what I most remember about the detour. A local hippie commune embraced us and our dog—until they discovered we were with the military.

As we neared Tacoma, Nathan was more excited than I'd ever seen him. I tried to sound encouraging and supportive about our future in the Pacific Northwest, but my body was a bundle of unhappy nerves and my thoughts raced. Though I'd assured Nathan and friends that I'd come to peace with the relocation, and I had to a point, a nagging sense of dread plagued me. It was as if I knew, deep down, that something sinister would find us in Washington.

We pulled into town and put our belongings in storage on the same day that we set up shop in an extended stay hotel since there wasn't any room for us on base. Nathan was so eager to meet his new squadron that after he'd spent only three days of our ten-day house hunting allowance with me, he went in to work. Though I begged him to take the time off that was given to him, he was so eager to get integrated that I finally sent him off with my blessing. To do anything less would be like making a kindergartner wait all Christmas day to see what Santa had left him under the tree.

It wasn't long before we moved into an apartment, knowing that within six months we would need to find a more permanent residence. Frustratingly, though Nathan helped me move a few things into our temporary place, I was left to do most of the settling in on my own because less than three weeks after our arrival in the state, he received notice to join immediately with his team down range on a mid-rip tour. That meant his unit was already deployed, and he would be meeting them in the middle of the deployment. Nathan's successor was in Afghanistan, and the only way to understand what he would be doing was to connect with her in the Middle East. He'd be gone for four months.

How overwhelming it is to be alone in a new city you haven't chosen, to know no one there, and to lack even a rudimentary understanding of how the area is laid out. *I'd rather be alone in England*, I mentally fussed as Nathan packed. Worse, I knew as I quickly kissed him on his way out the door that last morning that I couldn't just hide myself away in our apartment and live on the joy of regular communications with him. We knew he'd have fewer opportunities to contact me during the upcoming separation, and I had to find us a house and secure a job so that I could get down to the business of establishing a home and making certain all bills were paid.

Not long after he left, I began working for a beer distributor. While I don't even like beer, I was good at sales and knew a lot about the products. I soon realized that the work was a good fit, and it provided me a wonderful distraction. Beer never sleeps, so I rarely did either. Remaining on the go helped me cope.

The best part of the job was that it set me on a travel route that allowed me to learn the city's layout quickly. That knowledge aided me in figuring out where to focus my search for our house. Nevertheless, I found the task daunting. It didn't feel right to go hunting with a realtor without Nathan at my side. After all, it would be our first house together, and I certainly didn't want to get the pick wrong.

On a rare call with Nathan during this period, I expressed my concerns. He assured me that he would be happy if I was and said I could continue to send him online realty links that he'd check out just as soon as he could. For a moment, I felt better.

But then he said, "It's important you choose what you want, Jenny. A place where you feel comfortable. I'll only be with you for about two weeks once I get back. Then they're sending me to Florida for a month. Another training."

Which likely means they will ship you right back overseas after that, I silently fumed.

"Jenny, are you there?" he asked. He didn't know that I was pressing my lips into a tight line and trying not to scream.

I squeezed my eyes shut too and then forced a smile onto my face. None of the upheaval was his fault, and I wouldn't let our brief talk together close on a sour note. "Yes, I'm here, Nathan," I said as lightly as I could. "I'll be okay. I just got spoiled having you close for most of the last two years."

"I am sorry, Darlin'. I know it's not ideal."

"I miss you so much," I decided to reply. "Just get home to me, okay?"

He promised he would and that we'd eventually make many good memories together in Washington.

I chose to believe him.

8

LEFT BEHIND WITH A LITTLE EXTRA

"I hold you by your right hand—I, the LORD your God. ...
Don't be afraid. I am here to help you."
Isaiah 41:13

In spite of my loneliness, it didn't take long to decide Tacoma, Washington, is a beautiful place to live. I'm a beach-loving girl who feels that sunshine pours joy into a soul, but I came to appreciate residing in a place scented with damp earth and fir trees. And while the ongoing misty rain kept my hair frizzy and I had to layer up every time I walked outside, the majestic sight of snow-capped Mt. Rainier on the horizon helped to compensate—at least on the days when it wasn't swallowed up by fog. After a few weeks, I even started leaving my bedroom window cracked open in the evenings because nighttime's descent routinely brought with it the sound of gentle rain and a calming perfumed breeze.

By the time Nathan returned from the mid-rip deployment, I'd narrowed our home-hunting option down to one I particularly liked in Puyallup, which was near the base. It was not the prettiest house on the block, but it had character. And the fact that it would belong to us added to its charms. We signed the offer together, but then I closed on it with a power of attorney because by that time Nathan was in Florida on the training assignment.

Throughout that week, as I traveled to meet with clients, I spent a lot of time on the phone to move over all of the bills, turn on utilities, and set up reoccurring payments. On my lunch hours, I took care of things like filing the new address, overseeing the unloading of our storage unit, and directing the movers who helped me to deliver its contents to the house.

On the night that was done, I set to work making the new place feel as homey and inviting as possible while Barkley observed. I expected Nathan would join us soon, and I didn't want him to have to do much of anything when he got home. That way we could savor our time together. I had spoken to him longer on the phone during our four years of marriage than we'd lived under the same roof.

"Surely a day will come when he won't be deploying every time we turn around," I quipped to the dog as I hung a picture over our couch.

Barkley yipped, as if he agreed. But as I reached for my toolbox and headed up to the bedroom to hang another item on the wall, I realized that the fulfillment of that dream might be very far off indeed.

More long and lonely days passed, each rolling from one into the next without incident, until the morning came when Nathan arrived home. In my latest welcome-home dress, another red one with a gold bar at the collar, I greeted him with a smile and warm kiss. Together we worked to enjoy our new place and made the most of things, but frankly, our domestic life continued in a herky-jerky fashion because we had to constantly accommodate his travels for trainings throughout the rest of that year. We both knew such upheaval was just part of military duty, but that did nothing to make navigating it any easier.

By 2013, I was ready to start growing our family. And I can't begin to describe my joy when both the first pregnancy test I took to confirm a rising suspicion I had that April—as well as the second and third that my practical husband insisted upon—showed positive results. Nathan and I were about to become parents!

Yet even as I glowed with excitement over the little pink plus signs that signaled another dream come true, my heart fluttered with anxiety. Like so many military wives before me, I'd have to face much of pregnancy and possibly even our baby's arrival without my man at my side. He was scheduled for another deployment come July. That concern led to many sleepless nights.

"How 'bout we stop worrying and keep making the best of what I can be here to enjoy?" Nathan asked me one day after I'd moaned yet again to him about all the things he'd miss.

After that, I made a real effort to focus on the positives—at least aloud. One of the most magical came in early June at the sonogram office. While I was on the padded exam table, musing about how my belly was starting to look like I'd eaten too many tacos, I tried not to wince as the sonographer squeezed a warmed jelly-like substance across my middle. Nathan sat to my left, looking disinterested, though I knew he was just as eager as I was to know our little one was healthy. We'd agreed not to tell our parents our news until after this particular doctor's visit.

"Let's see what's happening in there," the blonde-headed woman chirped happily as she rubbed a little wand over my skin and stared at a black and white screen positioned at my right.

"What can you tell?" I asked, struggling to make sense of the wavy lines and dark spots.

She pointed to a rounded gray area outlined in white. "This is baby's head." Then she pointed to a flicker just below it. "And this is baby's heart."

I grinned, and she did too.

Beside me, Nathan was quiet, but I knew he was studying the screen with all of his typical analytic interest. Reaction would come when he was ready.

"Listen to this," the nurse said as she reached for a button out of my view. And in that second, the room was filled with the most beautiful sound I'd ever heard. "Lub dup, luv dup! Lub dup, luv dup!" sang our baby's heart.

Immediately, I started to cry, warm and happy rivers trailing down my face and into my hair. And when I turned my head and reached for Nathan's hand, I saw that he was just as moved as I.

Weeks would have to pass before we could discover whether our child was a boy or girl, but that didn't stop us from dreaming about how wonderful it would be to have either. I listened happily as Nathan spoke of hunting and fishing trips he'd like to make with his boy. Then he smiled indulgently at my excitement over dressing up in mommy/daughter matching outfits with my little girl. In truth, though, neither of us cared if we were having a male or female: we just wanted a healthy child to adore. To parent well. To teach about God, our generous Creator, and His love.

By the date of our gender revealing ultrasound, I'd been strutting around like a technicolor peacock in maternity pants for weeks—at least when I wasn't at work, where I felt obligated to hide my pregnancy under a jacket out of concern that it might seem odd to some were an obviously pregnant woman to run around town peddling beer. In spite of that, I was absolutely delighted at the thought of the baby's coming and practically burned with love for the littlest Nelson. I prayed over my tiny human daily.

This time I noticed as I situated myself onto the sonogram table that my rotund belly hid my feet from my view entirely. For a moment I felt like a blubbery whale, but then the flutter of the pink and blue ribbons Nathan held—one of which I'd soon tie around my belly to announce our good news—drew my gaze. *Stop that, Jennifer. All the bulk is a blessing. It's a visual reminder that God has sent us a wonderful gift!*

Soon that delightful lub-dup, luv dup sound again filled the room. My physician, Dr. Song, pointed to three little lines on the screen. "Congratulations," she said. "It's a girl!"

"A girl, Nathan!" I said. "A girl! Ribbons and bows and all things glitter and pink!"

He laughed, clearly as elated as I, and said, "Hey, now. They make rifles in pink! I'll teach our daughter to shoot straight."

For the remainder of that afternoon we were content, perfectly light hearted. I wore the pale pink ribbon everywhere we went and told my good news to all who would listen—including my boss, who was wonderfully supportive and said they'd cover my heavy lifting from that point out. But by the next morning, neither Nathan nor I could deny that a thundercloud was fast approaching to block out the light of our joy. In two days, he was to fly out to Afghanistan on overseas deployment 3. And he wouldn't return until shortly before the baby's birth—that is, if all went according to his colonel's plan and the little one's timing.

The hours that led up to our kiss goodbye were painful for me. In fact, I was sure that labor itself could not possibly be worse.

"Guess from here on out I'll have to go get my own Rocky Road ice cream, huh?" I asked quietly on our final night together in our bed. I rested in the crook of his right arm, my cheek and chin on his bare chest.

"Probably better lay in a good supply to avoid midnight runs," he said mechanically as he toyed with the messy bun of hair I'd piled onto my head.

"Kinda hate that you're going to miss seeing me at my fattest."

He didn't reply to that, so I shifted my leg so that it lay across his thighs and hugged him closer. Maybe he'd missed my teasing tone.

His hand dropped to my back and his voice sounded downright somber this time, distracted. "You'll still be the most beautiful woman alive, Jenny."

I gently squeezed him again and moved to kiss his jaw before settling into silence. I sensed his need to retreat an emotional step from the baby and me. I knew by then that it is something a lot of servicemen do to cope with the frustrations of having to leave their families behind.

"Dear God," I prayed in the darkness as Nathan caressed me and we both began to doze fitfully, *"just send him back to me with all ten fingers, ten toes, and his mental cognition. Please. Everything else we can figure out. Just bring him back to us."*

The next day dawned all too soon, and as I watched my husband go out onto the tarmac with the rest of his unit to board their C-130 that afternoon, my eyes welled with moisture. November, the month of his scheduled return, seemed so very far away.

The only good news was that for the first seven weeks that Nathan was in Afghanistan, we talked almost every day. That made July and early August more tolerable. But as that second month wound to a close, in spite of my best attempts to stay distracted with work, crafting, and taking long drives with Barkley, I found myself feeling edgy.

At first, I told myself the feeling was related to my pregnancy. Then I thought it might be linked to owning a home two thousand miles away from family and longtime friends. After all, while my local tribe had started to grow—particularly because we'd begun to attend a community church regularly, I still didn't know many people in Washington well. Finally, though, I decided my fears were probably best explained by the complexity of that particular trip. Rather than remaining on one base for the six-month duration of his deployment, Nathan was moving all over hostile Afghanistan. Sometimes days would pass in between the times we spoke. And when we'd close our calls, he couldn't tell me when we'd talk again, much less where he was going next or what he was up to over there. Operational Security standards required that he keep details to himself.

Frankly, though, realizing the source of my unease didn't help anything. What it did do was remind me to pray for my husband every time I felt anxiety's claws. At least a thousand times over the first weeks of September, I asked God to send guardian angels to surround Nathan and keep him safe. And I always followed it up with the same plea: *"Will You please just send him*

back to me with all ten fingers, ten toes, and his mental cognition?
Everything else we can figure out."

One thing that really helped me survive deployment three was a steady stream of handwritten letters from Nathan I found in our mailbox during that period. Each time a note arrived, I'd curl up in a chair—well, as best I could—and read those beautiful messages aloud to our girl. She'd kick and squirm at the sound of my voice, almost as if she could feel her daddy's love wrapping around her in my womb. When I was done, I'd carefully tuck each one back into its envelope and place it in a keepsake box I planned to give her. How I hoped none of them would prove to be his last words to her!

The missives to our baby, whom we had named Eva Blake by that time, were blessings I knew I'd long cherish even if they arrived in an endless supply and overran the box I kept them in. But the few video calls that Nathan shared with us were the greater gifts, refueling me on those long days when I just didn't know how I'd ever make it another hour without him.

On September 22, 2013, Nathan called on FaceTime. How wonderful it was to see his smile on my computer screen, to know he could see my own. The sun had just risen where he was, and he was about to head to work. He wanted to know all about the baby shower a friend had held for me that night. And how was my parents' visit going? Could I hold up each of the gifts to the camera so he could enjoy them too?

We spoke for ten minutes or so, both of us gushing over a dad tool belt he'd been given and all of the little pink-bowed and elephant-themed items the baby had received, before he asked to speak to Eva Blake.

"Of course," I said, repositioning myself and lifting my shirttail so that he'd have a good view of our growing baby bump.

I could tell by the surprised look on his face that he could see she was thriving in there.

"Hey, my Little Squishy," he said with delight in his voice. "Daddy sure does love you and can't wait to meet you. Take care of Mommy now, and don't give her too much heartburn!"

I chuckled at this joke I'd heard before, ready to move the camera back to its usual position to resume our conversation. But then he surprised me by continuing to address the person in my belly. For several minutes, Nathan spoke about how he looked forward to playing with her in the future. He mentioned teaching her how to play soccer or sitting in the floor and rocking dolls alongside her if that was more her thing. Hot moisture gathered in my eyes when he said, "Really, Love, it'll be your choice. I don't much care. I just want to be the best daddy to you that any girl could ever have."

All too soon it was time to say goodbye. It was getting pretty late by Washington state time, and Nathan said it was part of his day's work to prepare for a weeklong mission ahead. He needed to get started on that.

"You won't hear from me for a while," he said in parting. "Where my team is going, we won't have Internet. I'm sorry."

"I understand, Nathan."

"I love you, Jen."

"I love you, too. More than life," I said.

And then he was gone.

That night, just before Barkley and I headed up to bed, I grabbed a red velvet cupcake leftover from the baby shower and started to take a bite. But just before I did, I reached for my phone and snapped a picture of myself preparing to indulge the sweet tooth I'd developed and texted it to Nathan. It didn't occur to me that he might never see it.

9

UNWANTED GUESTS

*"I called on your name, LORD, from deep within the pit.
Yes, you came when I called; you told me, "Do not fear.""*
Lamentations 3:55,57

For me, our nightmare began at six a.m. on September 23, 2013, the morning after I'd texted Nathan the cupcake photo. I woke to the sound of Barkley frantically demanding to be let out through our bedroom door, which was well barricaded by Nathan's old military footlocker—as it always was when he was away.

I groaned and turned my head on the pillow so I could glance at the clock. "Barkman, you know the routine. You're three hours too early," I grumped while pulling the covers more firmly under my chin.

As if to reply, Barkley actually howled and even scratched at the door like he'd dig himself to the yard if I didn't hurry to help him.

"All right. All right, already!" I yelled over the deafening noise of his next yips. "Give me a second!"

I scooted to the edge of the bed and let my feet hit the carpet. I felt ungainly as I stood, my body heavy with the baby that was by now the size of an eggplant, as I shuffled to the door and shoved the footlocker away from it with the side of my calf. That morning my little security measure might as well have had bricks in it. The effort of sliding the box out of the way made me aware that I needed to visit the bathroom posthaste.

I opened the door and Barkley jetted past me and down the hall, making for the stairwell and yapping all the way. "Be with you soon," I said as I turned to go and address the sensation of having a fifty-pound weight pressing my bladder. "That dog."

That's when I heard why he was so upset. The doorbell was ringing. And apparently whoever was out front had urgent business, because they'd also started rapping impatiently on the door.

Annoyed, I took care of my needs while simultaneously trying to figure out who could possibly require me at that hour. The house was located just outside Joint Base Lewis-McChord; most residents on the block were military spouses. Since some of us had jobs that started earlier than others, I felt the most likely scenario I'd meet downstairs was a mom running late who needed me to provide emergency childcare.

By the time I started down the steps in my tee shirt and boy shorts, I could hear the rasp of Barkley's nails at the front door as if he were trying to open it. Vaguely I realized the house was chilly and that I should at least seek out a pair of jogging pants, but I decided that whichever girl was out there could deal with seeing so much of me. Stopping that infernal cacophony of barking, scratching, bell ringing, and knocking took priority.

Once I made it to the first floor, I covertly peeked out a window to identify the caller on my porch. It was at that precise second that my world upended forever. Three men stood out there: one of them was Phillip, our family friend and flight doctor for the 22nd Special Tactics Squadron. I would've been less concerned

101

had he been alone; perhaps his wife had fallen ill and he needed my help with their kids. He was a dear friend Nathan and I highly regarded as a man of faith and principles. But to Phillip's left was another man I knew to be Nathan's acting flight commander, Garrett, and to his right stood our chaplain, Nick. If that wasn't alarming enough, in the hands of both the flight doc and the chaplain were black-bound books: Bibles.

You're dreaming, Jena. You're just dreaming, I told myself even as my fingers pinched at my forearm. *Wake up! Wake up! You know what their presence here implies. That thing that's worried you every time Nathan has deployed. You're just imagining all this. You have to be. Wake up!*

But Barkley's continued carrying on and the cold of the floor beneath my bare feet agreed with the pinch of pain I felt. Inwardly I cursed. I was very much awake.

Horror rising, I felt my blood run cold. The early morning presence of those men really could mean only one thing. Something terrible—God forbid, something tragic—had just happened to my best friend, to my Nathan.

With fumbling hands, I turned the doorknob to let my unwelcome guests inside. "Not today," I said to them instead of the gentle greeting they deserved. At the somber look in their eyes, my ears started to ring. I fumbled for more appropriate words: "What happened? Tell me. Is he alive?" A hot tear spilled down my cheek as the trio of servicemen stepped over the threshold, and I wondered frantically, *How will I ever survive what's coming? What am I going to do?*

"Phillip!" I said breathlessly as I absently walked us all further into the living room. "What's happened to Nathan? Please, tell me what's happened. Is he alive?"

There was a horrible pause followed by the words, "He is, but we don't know for how long."

That grave admission hit me like a slap. For long moments, I just stood staring at Phillip, unable to speak.

The spell didn't break until he cleared his throat. It was then that I realized he and the other men looked decidedly uncomfortable. More uncomfortable than their mission alone would make them. "Jen, would you like to get a robe on before we explain what happened?" Phillip asked.

I glanced down, realizing I'd given them quite a show, and headed toward the laundry room to put on the bathrobe I'd just washed the day before. Oddly, I didn't feel embarrassed. My emotions were so overloaded that I'm not sure I would've cared had they found me bare as a mole-rat. Either way, I felt a depth of vulnerability that I'd never known before and couldn't process. It was terrifying.

When I walked back into the living room, appropriately attired, Phillip took my elbow and guided me to the couch as he and the others sat down around me. He began to speak, but my pulse was pounding so loudly that I processed only about every third word he said. Since I knew that what he was explaining was vitally important, however, I shook off the feeling and focused all of my energy on listening. The tactic worked for about three minutes, and I felt calmer. But as I processed, my whole body began to tremble and the ringing in my ears grew piercing. It was as if Phillip were speaking to me from the bottom of a deep well as a siren wailed.

The details he shared were grim indeed. In Ghazni Province, at approximately 7:20 a.m. on the prior day—well before I'd hit send on my most recent text to Afghanistan—the Taliban had launched a 107-millimeter rocket. It landed within eighteen inches of Nathan's head and had literally blown Nathan through the wall of a building. His injuries were extensive, and the few insights Phillip could tell me about them were enough to launch me off the couch in a panic.

No, Jena, I coached myself as the men looked up at me in alarm. *Don't you fall apart! Rely on the Lord. He's still in control, remember? Nathan's not gone yet. Hope is alive. You'll get through this. Keep your head. You're in command now. Be a good soldier.*

With a determined swallow, I dislodged a small bit of the terrible, sucking grief pulling me down as each of the visitors tried to calm me with whatever words he could. Honestly, though, everything they said rang hollow. I recall being vaguely annoyed that they weren't more help even as I appreciated that they were trying.

Perhaps sensing this, Phillip asked what they could do to help me practically in the immediate, and I mentioned that Barkley needed to go out. And I, ever hungry at the time, said I thought it prudent to eat. Yet even as I turned to the kitchen, the doorbell rang again. No doubt others on base had heard the news and wanted to offer condolences. But I just wasn't ready for that. "I'm going to make breakfast," I announced. "I need y'all to dismiss anyone who doesn't have the latest information."

Vaguely aware that Garrett was setting right to the task of answering the front door even as Phillip hooked Barkley's collar to his leash to head out back, I entered the kitchen and started a pot of coffee and preheated the oven. It was then that the tears streamed—slowly at first, then quickly growing into a torrent. As they fell, I got biscuits from the fridge, popped the can, laid them out on a baking sheet, put them in to bake, and set the jam and creamer on the counter. Then, feeling totally devastated, I moved to stand in front of the kitchen window that overlooked the backyard of a house that was glaringly far removed from many of my dearest friends. From the kind of normal family life I'd once envisioned for myself.

Eva Blake was due to arrive three months from that day, on Christmas Eve. And as I stood there at the sink, my mind raced with questions. Would I really have to face what should be such a happy occasion as a widow? Would I be the only parent to hear her first cry, to teach her to walk, and to attend her first ballet recital? Would I have to chase off the boys on my own? And for that matter, were mothers allowed to walk their daughters down the aisle? I absolutely did not want to ask.

"Oh, please, God. Let him live," I prayed in a whisper. "We've been married only five years! I cannot do this parenting thing alone!" And it was then that I remembered something I'd said to the Lord more times than I could count: *"Just send him back with all ten fingers, ten toes, and his mental cognition. Everything else we will figure out."* And I think that was the first time I realized just how tough a scenario I'd blithely offered to embrace.

I frowned at the rising fear for my own comfort that started battling with my distress over what had happened as I took the biscuits out of the oven. For a minute or two I continued to cry but also managed to pray for strength, reaffirming my willingness to do whatever my husband needed if only God would allow him to survive. Thankfully, by the time breakfast was buttered, I felt a tiny bit more at peace with all possibilities. While I knew I had some intense stepping up ahead and feared it, I was confident about two things. First, I really would remain faithful to my spouse and dedicated to his welfare: my promise had not been empty. And second, my God would meet me every step of the journey.

Phillip came into the kitchen then and asked what else he could do.

"When can you get me to Nathan?" I asked.

"I'm working on it," he said. "But there's a lot I don't know yet. I need time."

Time, I thought sadly. *My husband's life is draining away even as we stand here. We don't have time!*

Phillip attempted to redirect the thoughts that were surely all over my face: "Anyone you'd like Garrett to call for you, Jen? Someone who could come to stay here with you?"

Immediately Nathan's parents came to mind. Precious, far away Tom and JoAnn. Oh, how I hated to reach out to them with such awful news! I wasn't sure I could and was thankful help was on hand to at least initiate discussion for me. After all, their lives were about to be forever changed too.

I thought about how best to conquer that awful task and then gave Phillip my mother-in-law's number and a request for Garrett to call her. I knew my father-in-law would be at work and didn't want one parent to hear before the other, particularly since they'd divorced not long before that, so I said I'd call him. Because I could hear Garrett in the next room, kindly dealing with a new visitor who'd stopped by, I figured I had time to contact my own parents first.

Mom and Dad were still nearby at a hotel, having flown to Washington state to attend the baby shower earlier that week. Somehow I thought it would be easy to tell them what had happened, but when Dad answered my call, I found that wasn't the case. "It's me," I said. "Can you please come to the house?"

"Sure, Jen," he answered, sounding uneasy over the tremble in my voice. "Are you and the baby okay?"

I wiped my nose on a kitchen towel, suddenly aware that I lacked the ability to say much of anything about the tragedy yet. "Nathan was hit. Can you just get here?"

"Hit?" That word was nearly shouted. "Is he okay?"

"No. Please, Dad, just get here."

I received assurance my parents would be over within the hour, so I next dialed Tom, my father-in-law. By then it was a little after eight a.m. in Memphis, Tennessee, where he lived. The chipper, positive sound of his voice nearly stole my composure. My stomach knotted at the thought of grieving him.

"Tom?" I said, my voice small.

"How's my beautiful daughter-in-law this morning?"

"I-I-I need to let you talk to our friend Phillip. It's about Nate," I said. And though poor Phillip had just returned from passing my message to Garrett and was already on his own phone regarding the matter of getting me to Nathan as soon as possible, I shoved my cell into his free hand and fled the kitchen. I just couldn't bring myself to tell Tom the awful truth.

To his credit, Phillip handled the chaos smoothly. I heard him put his other caller on hold and introduce himself to Nathan's dad as he stepped outside. But though I felt momentarily relieved by this, I realized as I entered the living room that Garrett had already connected with Nathan's mom and was sharing the worst we knew with JoAnn. Devastated all over again on her behalf, I wanted to escape upstairs, but Eva Blake did a somersault in my tummy that underscored the importance of letting Nathan's mother hear my voice. For the time being, I was the closest link she had to her own baby.

I motioned to the flight doc that I'd like to complete his call. After a quick word of explanation to JoAnn, Garrett handed the receiver to me, and I raised it to my ear. "It's Jen," I said.

"Jen," she replied in her characteristic, calm way, "this is in God's hands. Our Nathan's in God's hands. Do you hear me? Now, I certainly don't know what His plan is here. But you listen to me, honey, everything will be okay."

"Yes, ma'am," I said obediently, knowing she was right even though I couldn't imagine anything ever being okay again. "I love you."

"I love you more," she insisted. "Now, it may take me a couple of days. They've got me working third shift at the hospital. But I *will be* at your side just as soon as I can."

At her promise, I felt a wave of exhaustion hit and wanted nothing more than to hide for the rest of the day. But I was due at work soon and realized with a jolt that there was another critical call to be made. Thankfully, just the thought of talking to my boss helped strengthen me. I was the company's special events coordinator and marketing assistant to my sales associates, and I'd discovered over the last months that I could be quite the professional when I put my mind to it. So, while the call would not be easy, I expected it would go smoothly. I'd just put on my taking-care-of-business persona. And sure enough, even when I explained to my boss why I wouldn't be able to attend work until further notice—which would prove a major complication for him and my coworkers who'd have to find coverage for the seventeen events I was to oversee—he sounded understanding and kind. Clearly, he too was eager to help me however he could.

After that, though, I knew I couldn't handle another moment of that wretched day until I'd first indulged in some serious alone time. So while it seemed all the phones in the house were ringing and buzzing all at once and people were continuing to show up at my door and trying to say nice things to me even though I could barely hear them through my mental fog, I walked away from all of it and resolutely headed back up the steps to my bedroom. Phillip and Garrett would have to handle things on their own for a while.

I entered the quiet of my room, having every intention of crawling back into bed. But suddenly that particular item of furniture looked terribly large and hauntingly empty. So, I changed course. I shut the bedroom door behind me, walked through the master bathroom, and into the roomy closet.

There I pulled every one of Nathan's sweaters from its hanger, tossing the clothing onto the floor as if to create a giant nest. When that was done, I lowered myself into the middle of the multicolored pile and pulled the fabrics to myself in big bunches. It was as if by doing so I could somehow hug their owner.

Only then did I give full vent to my aching, miserable sorrow.

10
NOT JUST A SOLDIERS WIFE

"The LORD is with you, mighty warrior."
Judges 6:12, NIV

One rocket is all it takes to change a life forever. But rarely does a successful rocket attack alter the course of only one person, even if it appears to claim a single victim. By the time I finally exited my room, dressed and as pulled together as I could manage, I knew that what had happened to my husband had also, in a figurative sense, happened to me and our baby.

With that realization came the awareness that I needed to step up immediately to limit our collective damages. I determined to retain my composure from that point forward. If I had any say in at all, stress would not be allowed to bring on premature labor. I also decided that I'd push to gain as much insight into my husband's situation as possible so that I could better prepare for whatever was ahead. And I'd do whatever needed doing to get me to Nathan's side. I had, after all, made promises to him and to my Creator that could only be kept if I refused to distance myself from reality.

"God, help me," I prayed as I walked back to the living room.

"Take courage. I am here," He assured my quaking heart.

I couldn't make eye contact with any of the dozen people who'd trickled in over the last hour and were standing around downstairs. One or two had come up to try to comfort me, and Mom had even offered a sedative that I refused, but the last thing I wanted was anyone's pity or something to dull my senses. I simply couldn't allow that. I wouldn't divert any of my limited energy to small talk either: at that point, I could barely breathe. So as I heard their murmuring conversations quiet at the sight of me, I determined most visitors would have to go.

Largely ignoring them until I could figure out a polite way to accomplish that, I went to my desk and started creating lists—much as I'd done when preparing one of my three-ring planning binders prior to a relocation. On one piece of paper I wrote down everything I knew about Nathan's injuries thus far. On another I wrote the names of anyone who might be able to provide me with new information; perhaps through the use of our social media network I could contact someone stationed in Afghanistan who could provide more up-to-date info than Phillip could. A third list was titled "Topics to Research."

That one was important because just the little I knew about Nathan's injuries at that point was enough to convince me that as sure as the military has its own lingo, the medical world does too. And just as I'd had to learn the basics of the former to feel confident among Nathan's coworkers, I'd need to know the basics of the latter to deal with his doctors. Though Phillip had explained that Nathan's back was broken in the t1-t2 region, that he had to undergo abdominal washouts to get the shrapnel out of his belly, and that his upper and lower bowel were being resected, I was unsure of what any of that meant. Even the news that my Nathan had required a colostomy and a stint in his ureter had left me with only a vague understanding of what he was up against. My ignorance scared me.

I was gaining momentum in my list-making when a surprising thought paused my hand. So much of Nathan's job revolved around analyzing intelligence, in cataloging and mining paperwork and files in the hopes of giving the U.S. a tactical advantage. And there I sat, gathering intelligence regarding my own upcoming mission in hopes that analyzing it would give me some kind of advantage. In spite of myself, I wondered sadly whether Nathan would live to do such work again.

The awful morning passed in a blur during which the phone kept ringing almost constantly. It seemed friends and teammates from every time zone in the world had heard the news and wanted to express support. While I appreciated their calls, the noise was unnerving; only the fact that a few of those check-ins came with new information from overseas made all the phone chaos worthwhile. That single-rocket attack really was felt by people all over the world. Some of Nathan's coworkers from Afghanistan were able to tell us a little more about what was happening over there. Yet because of the time difference between the States and their base, and because so much in the military has to go up one chain and down another before it can be passed along to the civilian world, it took a while before I really felt confident that Nathan—despite his extensive injuries—had a real chance at survival.

Around mid-day Phillip notified me I would be getting on a plane no later than the end of the week to head to DC. It was likely I'd be there at least one night while he finalized plans to get me to Germany. Andrews Air Force Base in Maryland was a mid-point where I could either intercept Nathan or make my way across the sea to Landstuhl AFB to meet him. My flying out to Landstuhl, however, would indicate that he'd likely not survive a move stateside.

"What do I need to pack?" I asked, aware that I had no say in how the next weeks unfolded or even what would be required of me.

Garrett stepped in at that point and explained that his wife Rebecca was on her way over to help me with details. She'd also aid in addressing the many legal matters I'd have to handle prior to departure. I knew Rebecca was the perfect person for that job because she was active duty military too. She'd been trained in Logistics specifically.

Things had grown awkwardly quiet while Phillip the doctor and Garrett the flight commander and I spoke, and I slowly grew aware that every ear in the room was awaiting what I might say next. So, feeling overwhelmed by that and still uncertain how to politely get most of those people to leave, I simply thanked Garrett and then excused myself so I could start packing basics. It got me out of that crowded room.

When I got back upstairs, though, I began to battle with renewed waves of fear. I didn't mind traveling; typically, I enjoyed it. But there would be no light-hearted sightseeing on this trip. And God only knew how much courage I'd need to meet whatever heartrending sights lay ahead.

Come on, Jena, I coached myself as I gathered a travel toothbrush and toothpaste, my hairbrush, and my makeup bag into one place. *You have been courageous enough to move all over the United States, to bicycle the busy streets of Chicago helmetless, and even to go to Bonnaroo by yourself when no one else wanted to go along. This Germany flight? You've got this. You can be brave, girl!*

But even as I tried to build myself up with positivity, I trembled. I'd need a lot more than personal courage to make this particular trip and to handle what was on the other side of it. I'd need a divine dose of strength and supernatural bravery. So, sick with anxiety, I turned to God again in prayer as I continued collecting items to pack.

This time my pleas for help were met with memories of a Bible story. One of my favorites. In the book of Judges, a cowardly man named Gideon is called by God to lead the nation of Israel against her oppressors. A vintner's son who had no aspirations of being a warrior, Gideon had to that point purposefully avoided the bad guys ravaging their land. He liked to play it safe. But when God sent an angel to visit him, Gideon stepped up. And he did it in part, I think, because of the way the angel greeted him. Rather than acknowledging his fear or the holes in his resume, the angel gave Gideon a strong hint of who he could be if he'd just choose to face the future with faith in God's ability to help him do what needed to be done. The angel said to Gideon, "The LORD is with you, mighty warrior" (NIV).

Still shaking, but inspired by the fact that nervous Gideon went on to live up to that lofty title, I stepped back into the closet and faced my rack of dresses. Because I knew Scripture, I had confidence that the same God who stood by Gideon would also walk alongside me. All complications aside, my Nathan was on his way home from deployment number three. And even though it seemed that this time I'd be meeting him in transit and it wasn't likely he'd know the difference, I would meet him in a dress and heels as usual. In my own brand of battle attire. To show the Lord and myself that I was willing to be the mighty warrior my little tribe needed.

Within the hour, Garrett's wife, Rebecca, arrived and gave me direction on what else to pack. I felt a surge of gratitude when she also handed me a list she'd prepared to help me know what had to be done before I could fly out. It was surprisingly extensive, but she assured me she'd walk through it with me.

We got in her car, and our first stop together was JAG, the Judge Advocate General's office. There I appointed powers of attorney for my home, vehicles, and so many more things that I barely remember it all. Afterward, we headed to the base where I wrote, as instructed, the names of the people I entrusted with my delicate affairs and made contact with each person who would be appointed as an acting interim. It was a complex process for which all paperwork had to be done in quadruplicate. And as I made decisions that day, it didn't help to know that my parents would be unable to stay in Tacoma much longer because of their work commitments back home. That Nathan's fellow service members and their wives kept proving so eager to step up in their stead was a huge blessing.

By the time Rebecca and I returned to my house, around 5:00 p.m., I felt a bit less rattled. Exhausted, sad, but more on top of things and therefore less vulnerable. The progress felt good. I had no idea I was about to face another blow.

Phillip met us just inside, motioning me to sit down for an update. It made me uncomfortable that so many people were still standing around in my house to eavesdrop, but Rebecca had assured me in our afternoon together that letting friends and family hear facts directly from knowledgeable Phillip might help prevent any spread of misinformation—something that was important to me since I hated the thought of our family being the subject of gossip.

At first, Phillip's news sounded good. Nathan's abdominal wash outs and back surgery had gone well, and he was stable. He was in recovery in Bagram Air Force Base in Afghanistan, which was a best-case scenario that we'd been expecting based on news that had trickled in throughout the day.

"So, when exactly can I see him?" I asked, hoping he'd report Nathan was doing so well that they'd moved up his transfer to Germany, which would hasten the timing of my flight.

But Phillip didn't answer right away, and that made me nervous.

"Phillip?"

He swallowed hard.

"Well, what is it?" I finally pressed, irritated because everyone in the room seemed to be focused on us.

Finally, he replied with a detailed list of internal injuries that were previously unknown to me. Nathan's liver, kidneys, lungs—practically everything in his torso—had damage. Yet even after telling me about all of that, Phillip still seemed to be struggling with how to phrase something else.

A sick wave of nausea rose deep within me. A gut-level knowing. "He's not paralyzed, is he?"

Silence.

"Phillip, tell me he isn't paralyzed!"

The answer came brokenly, as if our friend had all he could do to get the words out. "After Nathan's back surgery, they woke him enough to do a motor and sensory test."

"And?"

"As of now, paralysis is affecting him from the mid pectoral muscle down."

Paralysis. How that word bounced around in my mind, destroying what little emotional progress I'd gained.

"I'm so sorry," Phillip said, "but he … he currently doesn't have the use of his hands, Jennifer."

That did it. All the control I'd worked to assert publicly throughout the day and the measure of peace I'd found drained out of me in a moment and boiling anger filled their place. Right there, in front of my parents and friends and all those people who were trying to help but really couldn't because my situation was beyond us all, I began to cry. To sob with rage. And, unable to control anything else, I viciously demanded that they make quick work of getting out of my house.

11
INTERCEPTION

"Go out to face ... tomorrow, and the LORD will be with you."
2 Chronicles 20:17, NIV

I spent most of that first night and the next two days alternately praying, ugly crying, battling against letting worry overtake me, and then giving in to obsessive fear. Not until the flight attendant in Tacoma closed the aircraft door behind me and I was officially on my way to DC did I allow myself a sigh of relief. Soon I would see Nathan!

By the time I deplaned in the capital city, I'd decided my indulgent mourning period needed to be over—at least when I had an audience. Within hours, my mother-in-law, JoAnn, and my father-in-law, Tom, would meet up with me at our hotel while we waited to learn whether we'd still need to make a transfer flight to Germany, where Nathan had since been moved, or if instead he would be airlifted to the nearby Walter Reed Hospital. It would be the first time my in-laws and I had seen each other since we'd received our awful news. The first time we'd all been in the same space in two years. I determined to keep up a brave face for both of them, no matter what. Nathan was their firstborn, and in the past days I'd come to realize how horrible it must be not only to know that one's child is gravely injured but that his young spouse will be that child's caregiver from that time forth—assuming, of course, that the spouse doesn't desert. I loved Tom and JoAnn, and I intended to spare them any worries I could. While I knew better than to think I could avoid showing any negative emotion in their presence, I wanted to be a pillar of positivity for all of us.

I checked into the hotel that evening, and Phillip—who had flown out with me—called my room almost as soon as I put the card in the lock to tell me what time to be in the lobby. There he, my in-laws, and I would meet our SOC (Special Operations Command) care coalition liaison, the person who would be my guide throughout the foreseeable future. I'd been told he or she would help me identify and address anything else the military required of my household and would also provide up-to-the-minute knowledge regarding my husband's care.

After the initial greetings, the meeting with this appointed individual—a man named Alex—was a tense one; it was clear my in-laws and I were anxious and trying to hide it as best we could. And even Phillip seemed a bit haggard. Once we were seated, Alex began relaying what he knew. He again gave us his condolences and then spoke quickly and professionally, re-outlining Nathan's injuries and what had been done to address them so far. He reported that Nathan had been tolerating all the procedures well, but that he remained in critical condition.

"So we will need to go to him in Germany?" I asked, determined not to let my voice shake with the emotion coursing through me.

"Actually, he's on his way out of Landstuhl now. That's the good news: Nathan is stable enough to make the flight. By tomorrow afternoon, he will land at Andrews AFB and then will arrive at Walter Reed on a med-evac bus," Alex said.

"A bus?" I asked, the yellow-and-black school transport variety coming to mind.

"Think of a hospital and eighteen-wheeler rolled into one," Alex said.

Tom leaned forward to ask him, "Is there a chance he might be awake by then?"

"No, sir. I am certain they will keep him in an induced coma throughout the flight."

"Could you tell us what else to expect?" I asked.

To this he replied with enough new insight to tell me that while I thought I was braced for what was ahead, I'd need to up my game. Then he said apologetically, "Frankly, ma'am, you may not recognize him."

While I tried to get my mind around that terrible possibility, Phillip asked about the following day's schedule. Alex said something about how they were tracking Nathan's transition carefully and shared what he could based on the latest data, but I missed what else he said and knew I'd have to count on Phillip to explain tomorrow's general plan all over again. My in-laws would need him to repeat it, too. Though JoAnn appeared calm, likely because she had worked in the ER for a number of years and had learned how to school her face, and Tom appeared as stoic as I would expect Nathan to be were their situations reversed, there were hints of worry in their postures. Subtle signs of frustration that Alex didn't know more.

As anticipated, Phillip again proved himself a capable help in navigating our tragedy. He insisted we all just go rest that night, promising to outline the day for us the next morning. When the time arrived, he not only did what he'd said but also assisted us with accomplishing each task.

First on the to-do list was relocating me to Fisher House, which was down the hill from the main hospital at Walter Reed. It is one of a network of comfortable homes where veterans' spouses and families can stay for free while their wounded warriors receive medical treatment. Essentially three main buildings the size of fraternity houses that surround a center gazebo, Fisher House immediately reminded me of a resort surrounded by lush foliage and beautiful landscaping. There I would have my own room and bath for as long as I needed them, as well as access to a shared kitchen and television room where I could visit with others if I liked.

After we transferred my bags there, Phillip suggested we make a quick grocery run. I agreed it would be wise to lay in a good supply of peanut butter sandwiches and frozen strawberry bars to help address my constant cravings, and doing so gave me a tiny sense of normal in that otherwise foreign and frightening week. After that, he dropped me off at the Fisher House, reminding me I had only a small window of time in which to freshen up so we could go meet Nathan's ambulance.

Less than an hour later, Phillip pulled his rental car back up to the curb outside my new home; Tom and JoAnn were again in the backseat. As quickly as I could, I waddled out to meet them, wearing the royal blue dress I'd chosen for the occasion. I was a little embarrassed because I'd just realized that what had fit so well early in pregnancy was now hugging my swollen belly and breasts like a second skin. For a moment I'd considered trading it in for yoga pants and a roomy top, but knew I'd always regret it if I did.

I needn't have worried. Much later Phillip would tell me that as I made my way out to meet them, Tom started crying. He and JoAnn knew from pictures that I always welcomed their son home from battle in a dress and did so for the express purpose of showing him I loved, appreciated, and respected him. That the blue dress made their grandbaby's coming so obvious had only made the moment sweeter. It signaled that their Nathan's wife had every intention of standing beside him as always, of ensuring their family a bright future.

By the time we parked at Walter Reed and were led to the site where Nathan's gurney would be unloaded, I knew I was as ready to see my husband—injuries and all—as I could be. Nearly four days had passed since his accident, and I couldn't imagine trying to endure another one without confirming for myself that he was still alive. Yet how my stomach twisted as an ambulance the size of a Mack truck, accompanied by a full military motorcade, pulled up just outside the emergency room with sirens blazing! My in-laws looked as overwhelmed and apprehensive as I felt when the main vehicle's air brakes whooshed, and its back doors slowly opened.

Alex, who was standing just outside the building and beside us, leaned close to each of us in turn to relay the message that the walking wounded would depart first and then Nathan would follow. Just after that, as if to underscore his words, the ambulance ramp lowered and hit the pavement with a bang. That sound on top of all the others sent shock waves through my body.

One by one the wounded who could move on their own power, most battling some kind of mental or minimal physical ailment, departed the truck and were ushered inside. Afterward, there was a long pause during which I had to tell myself to keep breathing and not to pass out under any circumstances; beside me, Tom and JoAnn appeared tense and pale. A moment later a camo-clad medic gently maneuvered the tail end of a gurney out the back of the ambulance. As he and another attendant wheeled it down the ramp, I could see that a still form lay atop it. The patient was covered up to his shoulders in a quilt of red, white, and blue. And upon closer inspection, I realized the quilt was topped by straps tying the man into place as well as by several complicated looking medical devices that I couldn't identify and several IV bags of medication. Only when a total of six somber-faced attendants started to reposition the gurney so that it would fit through the hospital doors did I realize the man they surrounded was my husband.

As if to convince me of that dreadful fact, Alex leaned down to me and said, "That's Nathan there."

For a moment, I couldn't move. I felt like I couldn't breathe. As I stood there wondering whether I was suffering from shock, Alex stepped forward to speak with the medics, an action silently calling me to collect my wits. I could guess what was soon to be expected of me. The dark-haired man standing at the head of the gurney nodded somberly at whatever Alex said and then he and the others paused their movements. Alex turned back, seeking my gaze, and waved me forward.

As if in a dream, I walked to the head of the gurney and stared down at my precious husband's familiar but filthy brown hair, scuffed forehead, and puffy closed eyes. Tears immediately spilled down the sides of my nose as I observed that a nasal feeding tube, a breathing tube and mask, and a neck brace obscured the rest of him; Nathan looked awful. Having been desperate to do so for days, however, I bent forward and kissed him on the forehead in welcome, surprised to feel tiny granules of sand on my lips and by the stink of sweat and necrosis. It seemed that just as soon as I whispered, "Welcome home," Nathan was whisked through the hospital's doors and out of our sight.

Tom, JoAnn, and I, each of us feeling as if we were stuck in a terrible dream, were escorted through the main hospital and up to the surgical intensive care unit next. As soon as the elevator's doors opened to that floor, I saw a familiar form down the hall: it belonged to Nathan's friend and ranking superior, Chief Gleffe. The man stood there in that drab corridor like a tall pillar of strength clad in a red beret and green ABUs.

Still teary eyed, yet working to keep up a brave face, I hastily walked toward him as Nathan's parents followed. Nathan and "Chief" had been stationed together at Lewis-McChord, and he had deployed with Nathan and knew him personally. This friend deserved a warm greeting; no doubt he was almost as devastated by recent events as the rest of us. I hugged him.

Chief hugged me back, fondly calling me by my first name, and then introduced us to a shorter man who was also wearing a red beret and the standard Air Force uniform. His name was Colonel Kurt Buller, and to my surprise he also gave me a hug. He too, I discovered, knew Nathan personally. And it seemed he'd learned quite a lot about me from him and Thad Allen, Nathan's commander.

Over the next few minutes, as if on autopilot, I began to chat with the men even as Nathan was prepared for the move from the gurney to a bed in the room on my left. Frankly, I have no idea what Chief, the colonel, and I said to one another: my mind was focused on the unfolding action, which I could see with only my peripheral vision. There must have been twenty medical professionals behind the glass wall separating us from Nathan's room; some were dressed in military attire, and others wore white coats or scrubs. All of them seemed to be talking at once about Nathan's injuries as he was lifted, and nurses held his tubes and wires to ensure none of them pulled out or got coiled underneath him as they settled him onto the mattress.

When a nurse wheeled the empty gurney out of the room and along the wall not far from us, I found myself worrying about what might have happened had one of those tubes come out, which took my mind even further away from the conversation I was having. When I realized that and tried to cover the awkward lull I'd created, it occurred to me that Chief Gleffe and Colonel Buller were standing in such a way that they could see what was going on behind the window glass more clearly than I could. Colonel Buller looked pained by something he had just seen in there, and Chief's expression was one of horror. I'd later realize they had gotten a glimpse at the tragic sight hidden under the patriotic quilt. It had rendered them temporarily speechless.

That didn't register at the time because a white-coated doctor approached us just then, having come not from Nathan's room but from an office at the far end of the hall ahead of me. He was tan and dark haired and working busily to free a muffin from its wrapping.

"You must be Mrs. Nelson," he greeted me as he lifted the snack for a bite and extended his free hand. Vaguely, I supposed it made sense he'd drawn such a quick conclusion: I was a newcomer to the ward and the only one present who was young enough to be the spouse of a thirty-year-old soldier. He gave me his name as he chewed.

I nodded politely, keeping my hand in his no longer than necessary, and tried not to show my disgust over his lack of professionalism.

"I've looked at your husband's chart," he said before he swallowed noisily. "Injuries show that he is a quadriplegic with no hope of walking again."

At that bald, emotionless report, my mouth fell open even as he popped another bite of that stupid muffin into his. I felt my chest tighten with fury, and I narrowed my eyes on his expressionless face even as I heard poor JoAnn whimper at the callously delivered prognosis.

"I'm sorry," I said, though I wasn't in the least. "I missed what you said around the muffin in your mouth. Who did you say you are, and what is your position here?"

He repeated his name, which I would forever mentally replace with the more fitting moniker, Dr. Jerk Face, and said with a touch of pride, "I'm the neurosurgeon."

I froze, reminding myself that God sees assault as a crime and that we likely would need this obnoxious, yet skilled, man on our side. "So, you read Nathan's chart, did you? Congratulations. But tell me. Have you actually assessed him yourself?"

"No," he replied uncomfortably.

"Obviously," I retorted.

He cleared his throat and tucked the hand with the muffin in it behind his back. "There is a lot going on in the room, you see."

"Yet though you couldn't have done much more than glance at this patient who has just arrived, you felt it necessary to come to me—an obviously pregnant, worried, and scared spouse— to deliver your gloomy opinion about his future?"

He stared at me as if I'd sprouted fangs.

"A word of advice," I said, stepping closer to him. "Do not come to me, or any other patient's family in such a manner to deliver such news. Nobody cares what you think you can see from glancing at a chart, *doctor*. And I am shocked and appalled that you feel it appropriate to address me and my family while your face is full of food."

After that, he had the grace to quickly retreat, taking care to keep his snack out of our sight as he did.

My body still buzzing with tension, I fought the temptation to follow him, punch him in the nose, and throw his muffin against the wall. But that desire drained away when I heard Tom's chuckle behind me and JoAnn moved nearer to supportively squeeze my elbow.

"I'm sorry," I said as I turned to face my small audience.

"Don't be," said Colonel Buller as he stood there in a commanding pose befitting his position. "That little display of courage was everything I have heard about you. You are a fighter, young woman! And you're going to need fight to get through this."

The others echoed his sentiment, leaving me both pleased and even a little more frightened than I already was. It was the first moment I realized I'd have to advocate for Nathan's care, that he would need much more from me in the immediate days ahead than my mere presence. If I couldn't trust his surgeons to examine him before making judgment calls about his future, I wasn't sure I could trust anything. Such were my thoughts as medical personnel slowly began to filter out of Nathan's room and a nurse told us we were welcome to go in.

Leading the charge, I stepped through the doorway and over to my sweetheart's side, pleased to see his arms had been freed. That the straps holding him down were gone. I reached for his hand, for those beautifully formed fingers that had caressed my face countless times, and squeezed them gently.

"*Please, God,*" I begged silently as I stood there. "*Let those beautiful blue eyes snap open in humor as he tells us this whole thing was just an elaborate put-on. Let me hear him say, 'Hey, Darlin.' Let all of this awful go away this very instant.*"

Instead, Nathan's heart monitor beeped. His breathing machine hummed, clicked, and swished. And I stood there grieving, trying to come to grips with our new reality. It would be a long, long time before I would realize that sometimes God says "no" because His long-term plans are better than our own.

12
BE A BULL DOG

"God has not given us a spirit of fear and timidity, but of power,
love, and self-discipline."
2 Timothy 1:7

In that first afternoon by Nathan's side, there was so much
uncertainty. So much fear tempered by hope. So much noise from
machines and small talk and busyness as nurses came and went
and my in-laws, Phillip, and I tried to encourage one another. Yet
what awful silence came from our patient! No matter how many
times I leaned to my husband's ear to say, "Nathan, it's me. It's
Jen. I am here, babe," not so much as an eyelash flickered in
response.

At first, I was so horrified by this I didn't know what to do.
But slowly I refocused on the mission I had to carry out. My
American soldier needed my brave support, even if he wasn't yet
up to receiving it.

Not too long after I'd realized this, a young, blonde-headed
nurse wearing the standard Air Force uniform came to the doorway
and said to me, "Hey, Mrs. Nelson?"

I nodded, liking her sweet and kind voice. "Yes, please come in."

"I'm Lieutenant Miller," she said. "I'm the nurse in your husband's service today." Then she looked at Nathan and said just as kindly, "Mr. Nelson, we are just going to check your vitals." I liked that she spoke to him as if he were awake, just as I did. After taking his temperature and blood pressure and making some notes in a computer positioned on the wall across from me, she glanced down at a bag hanging beside the bed that I knew was filled to the brim with a murky, brownish-red liquid.

"What's in that thing?" I forced myself to ask, glad Phillip had taken Nathan's parents downstairs to the cafeteria for some dinner. No need for them to know the extent of my ignorance.

She paused and looked over the bed at me, smiled gently, and said, "It's a catheter bag, and what you've seen in there is urine."

"But it's so dark!"

"Yes, it is. But remember, he's had a lot of physical trauma and had a stint placed to repair his ureter. Once he starts healing, the urine will clear."

"And what's this on his chest with wires running over his shoulder?" I asked, pointing at a gray and blue box with a screen on its face.

"That's a wound vac. It's helping the left trapezius, an upper back muscle, heal."

I flinched at that. Alex had explained how that particular muscle had been severed by shrapnel, almost down to the collarbone. A few more millimeters south, in fact, and it would have blown the bone out of his chest and severed his carotid artery. "Could you tell me when we should expect him to wake?"

"It is really hard to say, Mrs. Nelson; he's been through a lot of trauma."

"But you don't think he's this far out on his own? It's his medications, right?

"The doctors want to keep him sedated for now."

I mulled that over for a moment as if it was news, trying to decide what else to ask as she checked this and that on the side of the bed farthest from me. "Can you tell me what meds he's on?"

"Of course. I'll print a list off here in a minute. But you'll have to ask a doctor what each one does when they make rounds."

I thanked her, studying her face and mentally counting her an ally.

She smiled at me, as if she knew exactly what I was doing, and said, "This your first baby?"

"Yes," I said, running my hand over my dress's taut fabric. "It's a girl. Eva Blake Lee."

She commented on how wonderful little girls are as she stepped back around the bed, telling me a little about her own family. When she was just beside me and could look me directly in the eyes, she said, "We will have to do wound care in a bit. If you are queasy, you may not want to be in the room."

I squared my shoulders, knowing she was looking out for me and also trying to gauge just what she and her team would be dealing with during the ordeal we all faced. "I'm not queasy, and I won't get in the way. I want to know *everything*."

Before the hour was out, I got quite the education. When Lieutenant Miller first folded the quilt down, another nurse removed bandages directly under it. Not only did these actions reveal the tubes inserted into Nathan's lungs to help him breathe, but they also showed that a twelve-inch long incision ran from my husband's sternum to his pelvic bone. I'd later learn that it was a surgeon in Afghanistan who'd made this particular scar: they'd needed the access to be able to wash the shrapnel out. The neat line was merely glued together because they expected they would still need to open it several more times to continue washouts. In time, a doctor would later tell me, they would stitch and staple it closed for good.

When the nurses rolled Nathan onto his side to change the dressings on his back, I did feel a moment of nausea. The man I'd made love with countless times was covered in angry, deep red bruises, and the gaping holes accompanying them—though packed with gauze—were like something out of a horror movie. The worst of these gashes were from two to four inches in length and soon sat open, like deep caverns oozing blood. Lesser wounds that were not so deep had stitches in them. Those that didn't, one of the nurses explained, had to heal from the inside out. Until then, each one would have to be cleaned with saline and packed with sterile gauze again and again.

Once I saw the damage for myself and had spoken with a doctor about its extent, I began to feel a pressing need to know exactly what had happened to cause it. Yes, I realized Nathan had been ejected from a building when it was struck by enemy fire. But what had transpired in the moments immediately after that? Had he even known what hit him? Had the first responders done everything that could be done to help him?

The next morning I went to Alex and Phillip with my need for more details as JoAnn and Tom kept watch at Nathan's side. Much of what they told me I'd heard before, but it was only then that I truly felt prepared to process it.

Nathan had been off duty, catching a few minutes of precious rest in the otherwise empty bunkhouse, when a rogue rocket screamed across the small U.S. outpost where he was stationed and plowed into the building. His injuries had been caused by flying debris as well as his body's abrupt contact with the hard desert ground where it landed. According to the official report, Nathan's ranking superior, Staff Sgt. Eamon Anderson, was first on the scene. Amazingly, he found Nathan up and walking around and digging in the still-falling dust and rubble for his IFAK, or individual first aid kit, so he could administer aid on himself. Knowing at a glance that Nathan needed more assistance than he'd find in that kit, however, the sergeant immediately ordered him to lie down and had to overemphasize what he wanted because Nathan couldn't hear him clearly. As Nathan obeyed, his brain began to register just how damaged his body really was. He could barely speak; his lungs had collapsed completely.

A medic had arrived by then and said he'd brought the chest seals the sergeant had been demanding as he called for assistance. The case file revealed that Nathan had been able to communicate to the medic that he couldn't breathe, and the man immediately began an infield chest decompression, which involves cutting into the skin between two ribs deep enough to reach the lungs and then inserting a tube to release fluid so that the lungs can re-inflate. Yet rather than being bothered by that pain, Nathan merely seemed relieved to draw breath.

The men worked fast to click-cut away his clothing and turned him over to start addressing the massive wounds on his back. At this point, the report said, Nathan was alert and fairly calm, but told the sergeant that his legs felt weird. Numb. About that time a runner was called to bring more chest seals: there was so much damage that they couldn't cover the holes fast enough and he was bleeding out. Before his ordeal in Afghanistan was over, in fact, Nathan would require forty-six units of blood: the average adult body contains only five to six.

To keep him mentally alert as long as possible, the sergeant asked Nathan if he knew what happened. He replied that he had awoken at 0705, looked at his watch, decided to roll over on his side and snooze just a few minutes more. In the next second, he'd heard the howl of the rocket, felt the explosion, and found himself being launched through the air before slamming against the ground. After that his ears were ringing so loudly and his throat was so full of dust that he assumed he'd have to tend his own wounds because he couldn't vocally call for help.

Nathan remained alert and responsive until the chopper came in to evacuate him to a nearby forward operating base for initial treatment. They stabilized his neck and loaded him onto a stretcher as he commented that his feet didn't feel quite right. Only moments later, he fell unconscious. By the time they got him on the surgical table, he'd flat-lined twice.

After the men walked me through all those events, I better understood both Nathan's injuries and what a miracle it was we still had him with us at all.

I hated that I couldn't undo what had happened, but I determined I'd do everything I could to restore as much to him as possible. At that point, though, I really wasn't able to be much help. Sure, I could pray over him and talk to him and show interest in his care, all of which I certainly was doing already. But I was still too ignorant to offer him much beyond that.

I asked Phillip if he could help me secure a Wi-Fi signal for my laptop; and from the moment he did, I began using the majority of my time to research specifics from ostomy care to each ingredient of the cocktail of drugs Nathan was on. If I wasn't up observing the work of the nurses or asking the doctors questions, I was sitting in the reclining chair beside Nathan's bed and staring at my screen. It allowed me to do something productive.

Prior to that week, I'd never given a topic like quadriplegia much thought. In fact, the only quadriplegic I'd heard about was Christopher Reeve, an actor who had once played the role of Superman and then later broke his neck when thrown from a horse's saddle. That's why I started my research on the subject by reading about him, looking for insights into what Nathan's life might look like once he got home—since it seemed Dr. Jerk Face's insensitively delivered prognosis would prove true.

After I'd exhausted that lead, being somewhat relieved when I realized Nathan had broken his back at a much lower point than the actor and would likely have more mobility than he, I felt better prepared to truly tackle the topic of spinal cord injury in general. The more I read, though, the more I recognized that what was done within the first days following an injury can have major impact long term. And while I'd nearly failed anatomy class in college and suspected anything I suggested to the docs might easily be dismissed, I quickly grew convinced that I really was as much a part of my husband's medical care team as anyone on that hospital's pay roll. And frankly, I had a higher stake in it than they.

A few of the physicians—including Dr. Jerk Face, seemed annoyed by my more probing questions and the tentative suggestions I made at first. But the patronizing looks on their faces or dismissive comments only fueled my fire. Others encouraged me, rewarding my efforts with respect and transparency. And one doctor in particular made me stop second-guessing my ability to advocate for Nathan's care altogether.

The head physician on my husband's case was a beautiful young woman with big blue eyes and shoulder length hair worn in a ponytail at her nape. Rather than making me feel like an outsider, she insisted that I call her Ashley from the moment we met and always spoke to me with warmth. When I asked her for the third time how much longer Nathan had to be sedated, she assured me that after he'd gotten just a little more rest he definitely would be awakened and assessed. This conversation prompted me to research a new angle: "sedation and spinal cord injury." Chasing it would change my approach.

As soon as Ashley left, I sat back down in my chair near Nathan's bed, put the computer in my lap, and prayed God would help me find insights. It wasn't long before I learned that when it comes to spinal cord injury, it is incredibly important to start basic physical therapy within days. This can change the course of outcome for many patients and also keep muscular atrophy to a minimum. Given that five days had passed since the attack and Nathan had been kept asleep for the entire time since, we were already behind schedule.

As the sun went down that evening, I sat in the shadowed room and considered the long list of heavy pain meds and sedatives Nathan was on. I also frowned, remembering how Dr. Jerk Face, who'd come in after Ashley's latest visit, had been condescending when I asked about whether all that was really necessary. "Indeed, he is on Propofol, Morphine, Fentanyl, Hydrocodone, among others," he said with his back turned to me. "But you must remember that one medication counters the side effects of another. We know what we are doing, Mrs. Nelson." I couldn't suppress the desire to roll my eyes. That was not a good enough answer for me. Moreover, only someone with an ego the size of Texas would say what he did.

Even hours later, the memory made me sigh with frustration. It was in that late- night moment that motion coming from the bed captured my attention. I immediately stood, heart racing, to see Nathan stirring the air with his splayed fingers as he stared, terror-stricken, at the ceiling. He looked as if he had just stepped backward off a steep precipice and was searching frantically for a handhold. Though I called to him and tried to calm him, it was clear that he was still asleep—apparently facing some kind of terror brought on by all those hallucinogenic pain medications and unable to wake to escape them. I'd read about that very possibility when I researched sedation and how it could react with his particular drugs.

The next morning was day six of the medically induced coma, and I went to the nurses' desk in the hall to report the night terror and to insist to everyone that Nathan be removed from all pain meds and woken immediately. I argued that such a drastic step was necessary both because of the need to give him the benefit of early therapy and also to assess whether he had any motor or sensory function below the level of injury. After all, if he were paralyzed as they said, he likely wouldn't be in pain and didn't need all the things they'd loaded him with—no matter how well intentioned they were. Only in getting them out of his system could the resident staff decide whether intravenous medications were required. If they weren't, the drugs were only standing in the way of progress. And causing bad dreams on top of his other problems. They had to go.

Thankfully, with Ashley's support, even Dr. Jerk Face agreed to do what I wanted. I was warned, though, that it could take days to wean Nathan off all those medications. That it might be some time before he came around. Even so, I became increasingly concerned he wouldn't wake at all as one hour passed into the next. I'd read that the longer a person is in a medically induced coma, the greater the chances for brain synapse degradation. I felt like we were up against an army of terrible possibilities.

JoAnn, worried by the increasing intensity of my vigil, approached me around dinnertime to say, "You need rest, Jen."

I replied that I understood her concern—my parents had told me the same thing when I spoke to them that afternoon, but I just didn't want to leave until he woke. "I can't go back to Fisher House until he's awake," I said.

She patted my shoulder, compassion shining in her eyes, and left me alone about it. After that, JoAnn and Tom and I sat in companionable silence as Nathan's breathing machine did its work and his heart monitor beeped. As seven, eight, and nine o' clock passed, we stared at the man in the bed, willing him to open his eyes and be the charming and vivacious Nathan we loved.

"Oh, God," I finally prayed in exhaustion as I stood up and reached for his hand. "We need some good news here." And for the next hour, my in-laws and I stationed ourselves around my husband, bowed our heads, and begged the Lord to bring him back to us.

13
UNEXPECTED BLESSINGS

"The Sovereign LORD is my strength!
He makes me as surefooted as a deer,
able to tread upon the heights."
Habakkuk 3:9

Two hours before midnight, I finally gave in to my in-laws' advice to take a break and go downstairs to the cafe for some food. I knew that afterward I'd have to head back to Fisher House for some rest. The tiny human swimming in my middle needed me to take care of myself.

As I walked toward the elevator on the trauma floor, I tried to stop wondering whether Nathan would ever wake up; I knew I also needed to quit obsessing over whether he would know who I was if he did. True, for all anyone knew, he could have brain injuries. But worrying about that would change nothing.

"Remember, you asked God to bring him back with his mental cognition," I told myself sternly as I stepped inside the elevator and pushed the button that would take me to the bottom level of the hospital. Thankfully, I was the only one in there at that hour.

I got to the café just as they were closing the kitchen, and I made a giant salad with all the trimmings: spinach, arugula, pita wedges, sliced chicken, hummus, and loads of veggies. That night my body craved rabbit food and lean meat, and I figured such was what Eva Blake needed. My own appetite typically ran to things like giant slices of pizza or bacon cheeseburgers. I paid for my food, ate it tiredly, and headed outside the building to see dozens of stars in the sky above DC.

For a moment I just stood there at the hospital's exit, breathing the fresh air and allowing it and the sounds of singing treefrogs and crickets to help work some of the tension out of my neck. Then, after a quick glance at the partially-lit sidewalk stretching before me, I decided my walk down the hill leading away from Walter Reed to the Fisher House would be safe enough and started for my temporary home. The property was a heavily guarded and gated military installation. The sight of such security actually gave me a pleasant feeling that night, helping to steer my mind away from the chaos that had consumed my life over the last week so I could actually enjoy the exercise.

Nevertheless, I found myself frowning over why so many people in my circle seemed determined to speak discouragement into my heart when I'd agreed to talk with them over the phone in the last few days, expecting—and needing—to hear words of encouragement. Was it possible they didn't know what a blow to my confidence it was when they'd say things like, "You mustn't overdo, Jennifer. Push too hard and you'll have a nervous breakdown" or "You need to be reasonable, Jen. You'll never be able to raise that baby and care for Nathan too. You need to consider all your options"? Was I the only one who remembered that marriage vows include a pledge to stick by one another until death? And if it were me in that bed upstairs, would those same people be encouraging Nathan to discard me quietly in a facility somewhere? I shuddered, realizing they would.

I paused walking at that troubling thought and shook my head with exhausted frustration, determining more firmly than ever that nothing was going to chase me away from my man as long as we both had a pulse.

I journeyed forward until suddenly, out of the corner of my eye, I saw some strange movement under the shadow of a tree alongside my route. I immediately tensed, realizing too late that I really should have asked Tom to escort me. After all, there were no cars on the road beyond the gate, and no other people were walking about in the middle of the night. Whatever was out there had to be an animal, and I certainly hoped it was a friendly one. If not, there would be little I could do to get away from it. Emotional exhaustion and baby weight were taking their toll.

Breath held and tense all over, I waited.

My stillness was rewarded. A young buck, having only a few points on his noble head, tentatively stepped into the glow of the street lamp above us. Immediately relaxing at the sight, I scanned the darkness behind him and realized that he was accompanied by four grazing does. Each one, in turn, raised her head and stepped closer to get a better look at me before continuing with her meal. After a minute or two, the buck crossed to the grass on the other side of the walkway as if giving me his permission to pass between him and the little herd.

Smiling and happy-hearted over this sweet nature scene, I continued on my way and soon made it back to my room. How I wished Nathan had been with me to see the little deer family! He would have thought their near presence on such a starry night was the coolest thing ever. And though the man loved to hunt, he'd always been content just to observe animals' beauty. It felt good to think of him in such a relaxed, normal context.

That night I slept so hard I didn't dream. And when I woke late the next morning to dress and head back to the hospital, I felt more refreshed than I had in some time. A week had passed since Nathan was hit, but that period had been so busy, heart-rending, and overwhelming that it felt more like a month.

By the time I got up to the ward, I'd prepared myself to spend another day watching for signs of awareness that might not come. After all, no one had called my phone since I'd left the night before. When I entered Nathan's room, I immediately saw that JoAnn apparently hadn't moved from the recliner where I'd left her. And still Tom was sitting in his favorite post at the foot of Nathan's bed. The only real difference was that Phillip, wearing his uniform, had joined them in the night as promised. And Alex was there too.

"Good morning," I said, making my way to Nathan's side and bending to give him a kiss on the brow. "Any news at all?"

"Actually, yes," JoAnn said with a wide smile as I straightened and glanced her way. "Nathan woke in the middle of the night!"

"He did?" I asked, looking down at his sleeping form and immediately realizing I'd missed the big moment by only short hours at most.

"He was asking for you," Phillip said.

At this, I felt moisture spring to my eyes.

"When we told him you were in bed already, he started to cry," Phillip said.

"Right after that, he went right back out," Tom added, likely trying to soften the blow of those words. Nathan was no easy crier. So to think of him waking in tears was painful.

I stared at my father-in-law, trying to smile my gratitude, even as my heart sank further. Had my Nathan thought they were making excuses for me? That I had deserted him when he needed me most?

I absolutely would not leave that room again until I had a chance to reassure him of the facts.

14
WHISPERS FROM GOD

"If your gift is serving others, serve them well. ... If your gift is to encourage others, be encouraging. If it is giving, give generously. If God has given you leadership ability, take the responsibility seriously. And if you have a gift for showing kindness ..., do it gladly."
Romans 12:7-8

Much later that day, Nathan's eyes fluttered open and his right fingers stirred. In the next second, I was out of the recliner and encasing his searching hand in my left one as I quickly moved to the head of the bed and leaned over him, thankful I'd thought to pull my hair up that morning. I gently combed back his messy locks with my free hand. The second our eyes met, his filled with moisture.

"I'm here, babe," I said. "I'm here and I'm not leaving your side. We are going to get through this."

Nathan stared hard at me. Then his eyes slowly widened before his eyebrows lowered in a gesture of hopelessness. I could see in that move that he was processing his obvious limitations, finding them horrifying, and wanted me to know how upsetting it was.

"This sucks, huh?" I asked.

He nodded once.

"Yes, you are pretty messed up," I agreed, "and I know this is difficult. But we've got this, babe." I touched my nose to the end of his. "I love you. I'm so glad you came back to me."

By this time there was no mask over his face, just a breathing tube down his throat and the other tube running up through his nostril so he could be fed. I noticed he was working his lips around the former, trying to speak. That he was telling me he loved me too was clear.

"I can't feel or move my legs," he said next, motioning in their general direction with one drawn-up hand.

"I know," I said.

"My arms are on fire," he said, although that message took me a while to decipher.

"Like pins and needles or heat?"

"Pins and needles."

I turned to JoAnn, who was understandably glued on everything we were saying to each other and asked, "Is this normal?"

"It sounds like neuropathic pain," she commented, stepping into his field of vision. "Is it shooting down your arms?"

When he nodded, she caressed his face quickly to comfort him and exited the room to get nurse.

As Nathan and I waited, I tried to reassure him that things would get better and that I would stand by his side no matter what. And though it was so hard not to cry, I refused to give a single tear release. I felt that if I broke down in front of him, he would know just how scared I was. How challenging his future would be. And that wouldn't do either of us any good.

What I'd not learn until much later was that as I spoke soothing assurances, Nathan was having a private talk with God. He told Him that while he wasn't certain what all was wrong with him, he knew nothing in his life as a Christ-follower could happen without a purpose. And that while he really didn't understand why he was in the situation he was in, because for a time he could recall only snatches of what happened, Nathan chose to believe God could bring good out of what seemed like a disaster. He also prayed not just for the restoration of his body, but that the Lord would guide him to live out his days according to His divine will—whatever that looked like. And he heartily thanked Him for the chance to be there to see me and meet his Eva Blake.

I wish I could report that my Nathan always kept such a positive outlook throughout his recovery. But the mountain range of things he had to overcome sometimes got the better of him. Not that I blamed him.

In those first days, it soon became apparent that my handsome husband was about as dependent on me as our newborn baby would be. Not only did the nurses teach me how to change his colostomy bag and pack his wounds, but they also insisted on showing me what to do when the bag ruptured and how to address a spot of necrotic tissue on his back. All of this, we knew, would one day be my job alone. Moreover, in spite of his chronic fatigue, they insisted that he push hard to do whatever he could—which meant I had to push hard to help him. And that was a tough assignment with my big belly in the way and constantly drawing me off balance.

Even as I dealt with my own exhaustion and learned how to cope with the worst of the medical challenges, we received a flood of visitors. Nathan's aunt and grandmother came to boost his morale, and William Noble, an old friend of ours, took a bus from New York to be with us. Many more guests came from the

Intelligence community, offering their well wishes and their appreciation for our service. Those visits, though, were always a little stressful: the Secret Service would lock down the hallway and the elevator just to bring a top official to Nathan's room. Because Nathan couldn't speak clearly with a tracheal tube down his throat—we'd opted for a surgery to position the breathing tube through his neck not long after he woke so he'd have more freedom—he was forced to mouth words and whisper faintly to communicate with his guests. My job was to watch his lips closely so I could verbalize what he'd said to our distinguished visitors, none of whom I knew very well and all of whom seemed the type to prefer formality and dignity at all times. Thankfully, it wasn't long until I got really good at this task, rarely missing words or asking Nathan to slow down.

After observing this manner in which we greeted guests several times and realizing it was taxing both of us, Tom suggested we get Nathan an iPad, thinking he might be able to type what he wanted to say with one finger. He could, after all, lift his hands. And it was readily apparent to everyone who spoke with him that his mind was fully intact—God be praised. Nevertheless, every attempt with the iPad failed. His hands could move but refused to cooperate with his efforts. The injuries had degraded them, and their fine motor movement was non-existent. Thus, for a while it was as if my husband was a prisoner within his own broken body, even when it came to holding a simple conversation.

Once the feeding tube was removed from his nose, Nathan could tolerate being propped into a semi-seated position, provided his blood pressure would cooperate. A nurse showed us how to manipulate the remaining breathing tube so that his esophagus could accept food. With that done, either JoAnn or I could hand feed him, usually tiny bits of ice or Jell-o before he passed his swallowing test. After that, he was allowed yogurt and deli meat too—provided we offered only small bites at a time. (Meatier things like steak would have to wait until the tracheal tube's removal and improved activity in his bowels.) Sadly, his neuropathic pain, intense discomfort related to the way his injuries had interfered with his nervous system, caused incredible agony that kept him from even trying to feed himself. He needed us to hold his cup for him while he sipped from a straw or to hold his spoon as he leaned in to take bites of one mushy food or another. Nathan hated all of this, no matter how necessary it was. And the resulting irritation on his face was harder to deal with than the task itself.

One day he snapped angrily at me over some aspect of the degrading and emasculating process of being hand fed lunch. I jumped, hurt by his tone, and said something equally rude to him. This was followed by a dreadful silence. I was thankful we were the only two people in the room at the time.

"I'm sorry," I finally said with a sniff of hurt.

"Me too," he replied, turning his face to the wall in an obvious attempt to disguise the depth of his feelings.

My heart ached for him. "Babe, we are just going to have to give each other some grace here. So if I do something you don't like, could you please try and tell me about it nicely?"

He looked at me, his big blue eyes just as beautiful as they were the day we met at the house party years before, though vulnerability had dimmed the confidence that usually shone there. "I'm not really mad at you, Jen. Just the stupid situation."

We agreed that from that time forward it was important we communicate whether we were upset with one another or the circumstances we traveled.

Every day I would sponge bathe him, shave his face, brush his teeth, and hold a tissue for him to blow residual Afghan dust from his nose. I'd also hurt for him, sensitive to both his pain and frustration. He was working so hard, but *everything* was a challenge. Even the constant visits from various medical professionals wore on him. I finally asked them to come to him during only certain windows of time because he simply didn't have the physical or emotional energy to handle their round the clock questions and tinkering with his tubes and lines.

Over the years, I've been asked whether I felt angry at God as I watched my husband's struggle in those first horrible weeks. I can honestly reply that I didn't. I knew it wasn't God who launched the rocket. As a pastor once explained, it isn't He who causes disasters. In fact, all the bad in the world is a result of mankind's insistence on rebelling against His love and desires. Yet in spite of the many ways the human race has marred His creation through things like war, and though even His most-dedicated human servants tend to forget about Him, God is the only One who can help us through the difficulties we face. The Bible says God *is* love, and He offers peace of mind and heart to all who will trust in the sacrifice and resurrection of Jesus His Son on their behalf. If we will but listen, He will speak whispers of encouragement to us through Scripture and through surprisingly beautiful moments within even awful circumstances.

One day as I watched Nathan sleep, I reached for his hand and studied his face. Though leaner and certainly more scuffed than I remembered it, it was just as appealing to me as ever. I'd adored it since I was seventeen years old; it was the face of my best friend.

"Help me to be what he needs me to be," I prayed in a whisper. "God, I'm not in this because it's the right thing to do. I love him. *Please.* Help me to live out that love faithfully. To love my Nathan in the kind of extravagant way You love us."

I received no audible reply to this request. Rather, I immediately had the glorious sensation of being wrapped up in a warmed blanket. It was as if I could feel the Lord's presence and a promise that He'd not only heard me but would help me.

In late October of 2013, about a month after the rocket blast, Nathan was moved to the Tampa Veterans Administration's Spinal Cord Injury unit. To get there, we boarded a small Learjet at Andrews Air Force Base. JoAnn agreed to follow us as soon as she could, knowing that the soon-coming baby was limiting my strength more and more each week. As they loaded him up, Nathan was on a gurney and still hooked up to IVs, a wound vac, and the ever-present ventilator. Two nurses accompanied him, and things were pretty packed in the back of that six-person aircraft. It was a long two-and-a-half-hour flight.

Still, I felt a measure of peace. Nathan slept naturally, Eva Blake kicked in my belly, and I watched the sights far below us from my place by a window. Deep down I knew Florida would be good for us. Nathan needed heat and humidity. His spinal injury kept him from being able to calibrate his own temperature like I could, and I'd been told that sunshine can do a world of good for someone who is mostly bed bound. It meant a lot to me that the Lord had provided this change for us: DC was already growing frigid. I couldn't imagine how cold it would be come winter.

We arrived in Florida without incident, and Nathan was housed in the ventilator unit of SCI for about six weeks. His primary doctor there seemed to think she could get anyone off of a ventilator, so long as it wasn't a necessary lifeline. She was tough as nails with her treatments, and it was so hard to watch Nathan go through it because he was tired all of the time and could barely breathe without help. He was also cold constantly, quivering and quaking as if suffering from hypothermia even without the added stress of having to work so hard. Nevertheless, with the doctor's assistance, he soon earned his freedom from any breathing assistance.

151

Once that was accomplished, Nathan was ready to start more intensive therapy. Each day the nurses would help me get him to the edge of the bed. And then I, round belly and all, would bear hug him into a bulky wheelchair before pushing him down the hall to whatever was on that day's schedule. The chair was such that he could recline with his feet up because when you don't walk, the blood in your legs has a hard time returning to the heart. It hurt me to see how swollen his feet were in those days because his blood preferred to pool there. "Just part of spinal cord injury," a nurse commented when I expressed alarm over it. Then she told me she'd order him some thigh high compression socks to help with the swelling.

In the physical therapy room, there was a 3D spinal column on display. During our first visit, Nicole the therapist gave us a quick guide of what to expect over the course of the next eighteen months. She talked to us about the fact that while Nathan had a t1-t2 split in his upper back, he also had residual swelling up to c4, a spot in the neck. Because each vertebra operates or controls something different, we would have to take this swelling into account as we pushed Nathan's body to reclaim abilities it had largely forgotten.

When I asked how much ability the therapist expected to see restored in Nathan's hands, she told me every spinal cord injury is as unique as a fingerprint. No two are ever the same. And because of this, only time would determine whether Nathan would regain any or all sensory or motor function in certain zones within his hands and arms, or maybe even below the level of injury.

"We start with the assumption that a patient will have to adjust to having a quality of life limited to his current state," Nicole said to Nathan. "Then we rejoice as a patient exceeds expectations."

From that first day, it was incredibly difficult to watch Nathan go through the therapy offered at the Tampa VA. Just weeks prior, the man had been bench-pressing over 150 pounds, deadlifting the same, and squatting over 200 pounds at a time. In that little recovery room, however, he broke into a sweat trying to pick up marbles and cotton balls to rebuild strength and dexterity in his hands. I could see by the storm brewing in his eyes after only a half hour of this that he felt humiliated, so I tried not to cheer too enthusiastically when his efforts proved largely successful.

"When can I lift weights?" Nathan asked tiredly when Nicole announced he was finished with that morning's session. "I saw a guy with injuries like mine working on a weight machine on the way in. This marbles thing sucks."

Nicole smiled. "I'm happy to let you try that later this week, but first you need grip strength—thus the marbles."

Four mornings later Nathan didn't even want to get out of bed. He was sad and depressed and sore in his neck and shoulders from days of therapy efforts. In the nearly two months since injury, he'd dropped more than seventy pounds due to muscular atrophy. I'd never seen him so down emotionally. He wouldn't even eat his breakfast of bacon and toast without me coaxing him as if he were a fussy toddler.

Weariness washed over me when Marc, the gentle Brazilian man who was also Nathan's Occupational Therapist, stepped into the room to announce that that day's work would be done in Nathan's room. Given how surly my husband was that morning, I expected I was about to witness a battle of wills.

"What's on the agenda today?" I asked, moving Nathan's tray of food so I could stand and Marc and I could trade places beside him.

Marc grinned good-naturedly and held up what looked like a couple of long Velcro straps and two silver utensils. "Today, my man," he said as he reached for Nathan's right hand, "you learn how to feed yourself again."

Nathan shut his eyes firmly and turned his head away from Marc, refusing to acknowledge the device Marc was strapping to his palm—essentially a resting place that would steady a specially handled spoon or fork so he could eat on his own even without further gains in dexterity. "Get this thing off me," he insisted crossly even as Marc wheeled the tray of food closer.

Meanwhile, I started praying. Within short weeks, I'd have Eva Blake to care for too. Surely my husband didn't expect me to hand feed him for the rest of his life—not if it was something he could do for himself if only he'd cooperate. With a shudder, I tried not to imagine sitting at the dinner table while nursing my daughter and spoon-feeding my husband in between trying to eat bites of my own cold meal. I was willing to do whatever was necessary, but I sure needed Nathan to step up where he could.

"Come on, man," Marc cajoled, insisting he'd seen this device work wonders and knew Nathan would appreciate the freedom it would give him. "Give it a try. You'll be glad you did."

After a couple of minutes of Marc's ongoing encouragement and sunny positivity, Nathan slowly fixed steely eyes on him and snapped, "Okay, fine. Just shut up and teach me what to do."

Before the week was out, Nathan could not only feed himself but also managed to lift one-pound weights down in the physical therapy room. And while he absolutely hated all of it, he did whatever was asked of him to the best of his ability from that point forward.

Slowly, and with plenty of setbacks and more than a few exhausted sobs, Nathan got a bit stronger. He was able to get out of his bed and into his wheelchair without dizziness, and he could sit up straight rather than having to be leaned back. He also moved up to three-pound weights and conquered those blasted marbles and cotton balls completely. Yet while he made vast improvements, we both recognized we could never return to our home in Tacoma. Neither the two-story house nor its steep driveway would be able to accommodate the wheelchair we'd come to accept would henceforth be a part of our lives. We knew we would have to sell the property and have whatever we could shipped to wherever we finally landed—likely someplace warm and certainly a spot close to ongoing, quality medical care. "It's time to make the call," Nathan said one day after a long discussion on finances. "Go ahead and sell the house in Tacoma."

At that point, JoAnn and I were living in the local La Quinta Inn. We were using the shuttle to get back and forth to the hospital, and it was becoming increasingly wearing to be without my own car and all of my own things—including Barkley, who I'd not seen in weeks. Though there was still much I didn't know, it was time to take some tentative steps out into our future.

Soon the realtor from whom we had purchased our Washington house listed it for us. Since we were still in contact with the squadron back in Tacoma, they agreed to facilitate and oversee and shipping of our things to help. But I was hesitant to let them handle moving my Jeep across country without a driver. If the military did that, it would mean our final permanent change of station would be to MacDill Air Force Base in Tampa. And since we weren't sure that's where we wanted to live long term, it was an arrangement that made me uncomfortable. Ultimately, I decided to break into our nest egg. I knew it was important to strategize and stretch every saved dollar in that season in which I couldn't work, but I felt that my vehicle's transport was one thing I'd just have to cover—if I could figure out who to contact about it.

As I was sitting by Nathan and praying about the shipping matter one day while he napped, a sweet representative from America's Fund stopped by. She told me that initially, she'd come to deliver me a basketful of baby items: blankets, bottles, diapers, and more. These she set in my lap, and I smiled as I thanked her. But she said that after she'd spoken to the nurses about my situation, she felt compelled to offer her personal assistance too if needed. Was there anything she could do for me?

I stared at her for a moment after she said that, wondering whether God had sent an actual angel right when I needed one. But no. She looked entirely human to me—and was, after all, representing a charity I knew of. "Actually, yes," I said. "I do wonder whether you could help me. You see, I need to ship our Jeep Patriot down here from Washington state, and I was just sitting her thinking that I don't know who to trust with the transit since I've never done a vehicle move before."

Her face lit with a big smile as she bent at the waist and reached forward to pat my knee. "Honey, let me take care of it. That is too easy for an old moving pro like me."

Sure enough, within ten days, I had my car and more freedom than I'd had since the flight to Washington weeks before. And not only was I delighted to realize the visitor really had stepped up to help me in the matter, but she'd enlisted the support of the transit company. Out of compassion for our situation, they donated their services and hauled our car across the country for free. The invoice I'd been handed that morning said, "Paid in Full. Thank you for your service to our country."

The first time I got behind the Jeep's steering wheel, I rolled down the windows and sat for a minute in the warm sunshine. "Thank You, God," I said. "Thank You for every

156

blessing large and small. For sending us just who've needed at every turn in the road so far. I am so grateful, Lord, for the way You use people to help others."

15
THEN THERE WERE THREE

"Children are a gift from the LORD; they are a reward from him.Children born to a young man are like arrows in a warrior's hands."
Psalm 127:3-4

In Tampa, weeks began to jet by at an alarming rate—particularly because local obstetricians were reluctant to take on a new patient so far along in her pregnancy. While Nathan continued to gain ability and strength and even mastered the use of an electric wheelchair that he could propel with a hand lever, I searched for a doctor. Finally, with God's help, I stumbled across the petite and kindly Dr. Dill, whose practice took me with open arms even though they were unaware of what awful circumstances had brought us to Florida in the first place. (Frankly, I didn't want preferential treatment due to Nathan's injury. Because I was desperate for some semblance of normal in my chaotic life, I really wanted to be addressed just like any other patient about to birth her first child.)

On the morning of December 20, 2013, I arrived at the VA after a night at my new apartment where Barkley would anxiously wait for my return: most of our things were in storage nearby. I'd been putting off most of the unboxing to accommodate all the other things demanding my attention. How thankful I was on that balmy day so close to Christmas that I could do life without a bulky coat: it was eighty degrees outside and beautifully sunny. I was wearing black yoga pants, a tank top, and a lightweight wrap—my typical late pregnancy attire. And if I were honest with myself, I realized that I'd just as soon forego winter weather for the rest of my life if Nathan opted to stay in the area long term as I was beginning to expect he would.

It was around 8:00 a.m., and while things were going according to my usual schedule and I'd stopped by Starbucks for breakfast as always, things felt a little off. For instance, on that day the distance from the parking lot, through the hospital's entrance, and down the long corridors to Nathan's side might just as well have been three football fields of swampy ground to cover. My body felt heavy and tired; worse, my hands were bothering me, and I kept dropping the sack containing Nathan's requested cheese Danish. Over the last few weeks, I'd developed carpal tunnel: my own fingers had grown numb and clumsy.

JoAnn met me in Nathan's room, having just smoothed the bedding on the air mattress where she'd slept the night. How thankful I was to have her there: over the long months of working together on Nathan's behalf, her cool, collected personality and easy conversation helped to soothe me.

I put the Danish on Nathan's bed table as he began to stir. I wasn't in pain, but I didn't feel right either, so I said, "Could you help Nathan get going this morning before you head out, Mama Jo? I don't think I have the strength."

"Sure, baby," she said, motioning me over to the air mattress. "Come lay down and prop your feet up. It's normal to feel that way at this phase."

I did as she said, staring up at the ceiling as she took Nathan through his morning hygiene routine. I must've started dozing during it because the next thing I knew, he was sitting in his wheelchair beside me and looking down on me with concern.

With an ear-to-ear smile, he softly said, "Good morning, beautiful. I'm sorry you're feeling tired today."

I gave him a look to suggest I felt he was mocking my fat form.

"No, I'm serious," he said with a twinkle in his eye. "I am more in love with you now at this very moment than I ever thought I could be."

At this, I smiled and reached up to take his hand. We had been through so much together. Our lives had changed drastically. Yet we'd remained partners, somehow falling even harder for one another because of our struggles. "I love you, too," I said.

Nathan's glance moved to my middle. "I am *so* excited about meeting our baby girl in three days."

"If she waits until then," I quipped as I freed his fingers and smoothed both of my hands over my belly.

He looked concerned. "Do you think it will happen sooner?"

"I don't know. I've never been pregnant before. But somehow, today I feel different. Like I just have to rest."

That's the last thing I remember about that morning because I managed to sleep in that spot for over seven hours after he left for therapy and during whatever else he did that day. When I woke to feel Nathan grazing his fingertips across my forehead from his chair that was again beside me, I realized I was famished.

"I need steak and a sweet potato," I announced as I rolled myself up and into a somewhat seated position.

Nathan laughed heartily at that; my appetite had been growing as fast as my gut. It just so happened that since we'd planned for the baby to come that weekend, we were scheduled to take my sister-in-law, Amanda, and niece, Zoe, to Outback Steakhouse that night. In preparation, we'd rented a wheelchair accessible van for a few days and had secured Nathan clearance from the doctors for a weekend pass. Also, the nursing staff had packed us with a Nathan "GO-bag" full of medications, cath kits, ostomy supplies, a blood pressure cuff, and a heart monitor to make sure he didn't overdo on his first post-injury break from hospital life. It was so important to him that he not miss anything related to Eva Blake's coming, including this anticipatory dinner we'd all worked extra hard to make possible.

Soon our little group, visitors included, was loaded up in the rented van—the nurses having made sure to give Nathan the extra support of a C-collar for our excursion, and we journeyed the two miles from the VA to Outback. Mama Jo was driving; I was in the front passenger's seat; and Nathan and the others sat behind us.

As soon as we arrived, I got out and opened the sliding van door so we could unload Nathan. I crouched down beside his chair to unbuckle his safety harness, my stomach gurgling loudly. And that's when I felt it. A rush of warm water spilled out from between my legs and splashed my shoes.

Surprised, I took my hands off the harness and said with a chuckle, "Hey, y'all: I don't think we're eating here tonight."

Nathan looked down at me, perplexed, and JoAnn asked why not. The rest of the family expressed similar confusion. We had, after all, been planning this evening for days.

"Either my water just broke," I said, "or I involuntarily peed myself, which would mean we've got another problem entirely." I stood clumsily as they stared in shock, and I felt my midsection tighten slightly. The sensation nearly stole my breath. Eva Blake squirmed, as if to affirm that her arrival was imminent.

"Let's get you back in the van," JoAnn said. Since the ramp to lower Nathan's chair was down already, I made my way into the back to sit next to my niece Zoe. She was five at the time. Mama Jo knew as well as I did that we'd have to run back to the VA to pick up the baby's-coming-luggage from my Jeep and the Go Bag we'd left sitting in Nathan's room, before heading over to St. Joseph's Hospital for the birth.

Soon, while my mother-in-law practically ran to gather my bags and to let Nathan's nurses know we were on the official countdown to the big event they'd awaited with us, I sat enduring contractions as Nathan timed them by looking at the smartphone timer in his lap. I'd not had time or energy for birthing classes, so I worked my way through my pains with yoga breathing. Nathan sat in amazement as I did, both because of how calm I appeared and because things were progressing so quickly.

Little Zoe finally asked, "Aunt Jena, does it hurt?"

"No," I said as I smiled at her reassuringly. "Eva Blake is just taking my breath away a little."

By the time we pulled up to St. Joseph's, my husband was excitedly saying, "They are six minutes apart now. You're doing great, Jen!" JoAnn helped me out of the car and then went to unstrap Nathan's chair and get it down to pavement level. As I waited, I stood in place and rubbed my lower back, gently shifting my weight from one foot to the other. I wasn't moaning or yelling like the laboring women in movies. Instead, I welcomed what I saw as the beauty of each contraction. Every single one was like a jolt of electricity getting me closer to the moment when I'd meet my little girl.

When JoAnn and the others hustled away to park the van, I waddled myself through the hospital's front doors as Nathan rolled along behind me in his electronic wheelchair. Every few steps, I had to pause for a contraction, bending slightly at the waist and placing my hands on my knees. When I, trembling both from exertion and excitement, finally reached the clerk at the front desk, I explained that I was in labor and asked what I needed to do to check in. Things were happening so fast that I worried I might give birth in the waiting area.

To my relief, we were ushered into a birthing room, which looked very much like a well-appointed room in a Ritz-Carlton. A nurse gave me a gown to change into, explained what to expect as she waited for me to put it on behind a curtain, and helped me onto the birthing table. Already I was at six centimeters. A half hour later, I'd reached eight. I didn't fight it when she put an IV in the back of my hand, nor did I argue when she suggested an epidural.

"I hear we are about to have a baby," Dr. Dill said when she arrived at the foot of the table a few minutes later, wearing a yellow paper gown and mask.

I nodded to this as Nathan introduced himself. As they spoke, I concentrated on my breathing as my middle tightened— this time a bit harder. When the squeezing sensation let up, I said, "It'll be the twenty-first day of the twelfth month in minutes, Doc. I'd like to be able to say she was born at 12:21am too. That would be fun." I hoped having a short-term goal like that would help me to get through the intensifying inner squeeze-waves that were rising, peaking, and subduing again like waves on a beach.

She adjusted the sheet that was over my bare legs and checked my progress herself. "Baby Girl will be here anytime now," she said with a smile lighting her eyes.

I sighed at this, realizing there likely wouldn't be time for Amanda, who'd gone out to grab all of us some food, to get back to us before the big arrival. But as I thought on it, I realized that was okay by me. Mama Jo and Zoe already sat observing at my side, and it was bad enough to have the doctor and nurse staring at my southern regions. How anyone could bear to have a roomful of familiar faces focused intently on things down there blew my mind.

I was just starting to forget this fresh embarrassment over my exposed position and concentrate on pushing—which suddenly seemed like a great idea—when Nathan made an announcement: "I want a front row seat for this."

For a moment, I was tempted to protest. But then I started to laugh and granted him permission—after all, he'd almost missed the day altogether. It was only fair that after having endured my constant observation in his most exposed moments over the last few months, he should be allowed to do what he wanted in our delivery room.

"Fine by me," laughed Dr. Dill. She then motioned to a spot partly behind and beside her where he'd have a great view. By this point, she was fully aware of the circumstances that had brought us to her practice. We had talked at length over the last few weeks of office visits, and I'd filled her in on things. Still, it was a relief to see that she really wasn't at all rattled to find my husband in a wheeled chair and C-collar.

After Nathan maneuvered his chair into the place indicated, things happened in a blur. I remember a moment of discussion regarding how they could help Nathan catch the baby given that his arms were still compromised, and his hands hadn't regained full strength. Once that plan was in place, Nathan began telling the doctor and nurse funny stories about our long history together. Throughout the rest of the labor, in fact, he had me laughing so hard between contractions that I almost forgot there had ever been a blast in Afghanistan, that we'd spent the last three months of our lives in hospitals. I thought only about how much I loved my husband and how thrilled I was to be pushing our child into the world.

Before the rocket attack, Nathan had always been able to steer my thoughts away from frustrating or painful things when he set his mind to it. After it, I would notice over time, he seemed to hone this power of positive engagement and diversion not just for my own benefit but for that of others. This was, I'd come to realize, the first of many divine gifts to the world that would rise from his ordeal.

Precisely six hours after my water broke, and just shy of 12:21 a.m., I heard the most breathtaking sound in the world: our daughter's first cry. Eva Blake Nelson was rosy and round-cheeked and the sight of her in Nathan's arms, supported by the nurse's, filled me with joy. We'd soon learn she was seven and half pounds and nineteen inches in length. **Absolutely perfect.**

For three glorious days, I was able to rest there at St. Joseph's and to focus exclusively on my daughter. To marvel over tiny hands, miniature toes, the O shape she made with her little pink mouth, and the wonderful fact that mine was now a family of three. I wanted to relish the quiet and singular focus while I had it, while Nathan and Mama Jo were back at the VA and my world was no bigger than my own hospital room. Yet, if I'm honest, anxiety never quite left my side. My complicated life, I knew, had just gotten far more tangled.

16
TIME TO GO HOME

"You have armed me with strength for battle."
Psalm 18:39

On Christmas Eve, I pushed Eva's stroller down the hallway toward Nathan's room at the VA. It was our first time out of St. Joseph's, and it seemed that every nurse, doctor, therapist, and custodian in the Spinal Injuries department stopped me along the way, offering congratulations and compliments galore. Everyone lit up with joy at the sight of my little bundle. Even many of the long-term patients sent requests through their nurses, asking that I bring her by to visit as soon as I could. Eva Blake Nelson was a visual reminder that miracles and good things still happened in the world.

The ward had a cheerful feel that afternoon—not just because of the baby's arrival but because during the holidays, various veteran organizations worked hard to bring Christmas to those who couldn't go home to enjoy it. The aroma of traditional Christmas fixings, for instance, permeated the long hallway since several well-wishers walked the hospital corridors to deliver either home-cooked hot meals or blankets and goody bags full of toiletries. The nurses had put a miniature Christmas tree on their station counter, and everyone was wearing Santa hats or cheerful holiday jewelry.

"Make sure you don't miss The Semper Fi Fund's dinner tonight, Mrs. Nelson," Nicole the therapist said just after she'd marveled over my baby for a good five minutes. "They are catering in a feast with all of the trimmings, and I hear Mr. and Mrs. Clause will be handing out presents."

I thanked her for the tip, promising we would attend, and then maneuvered the stroller into Nathan's room. He was thrilled to see us again but needing a nap. It would take him a while to recover fully from that weekend's outing.

"How 'bout I snuggle Eva here on the bed while I rest?" Nathan asked hopefully, and JoAnn immediately stepped in to say she couldn't see why not. I agreed. After all, his hospital bed had rails on its sides and my mother-in-law and I would be right there.

I pushed a button to recline the mattress and help Nathan get settled as JoAnn took Eva Blake from her car seat that clicked into the stroller and then shoved the bulky conveyance out of the way against a wall. Since I'd just fed the baby before we'd entered the hospital, I figured we'd have at least an hour before she'd start rooting for food. It made me smile to realize that the crook of Nathan's arm would make a perfect little nest for her to sleep in. He looked so satisfied as JoAnn settled her there. His "Little Squishy" was against his ribs where she would feel the beat of his heart.

Just before he drifted off to sleep, Nathan shared his bad news. "They tell me I shouldn't have worn my shoes all night in the hospital on Friday," he said. "I've developed two deep tissue injuries: one on each heel. They're pretty rough."

As he dozed off, JoAnn explained that since he'd been in his tennis shoes up until the birth and another six hours after that, we did indeed have a new set of wounds to address. It was not the kind of report that encourages a girl.

By the day after Christmas, all of the excitement of the last week plus learning how to address the awful new injuries was catching up with me. I was emotionally spent. And while Eva Blake was one of those rare babies that seldom cries, I'd already begun to gain a sense of what my new normal was to be: exhausting on every level.

Nathan, by contrast, got a new wind of enthusiasm for recovery as the new year, 2014, drew closer. "I've been giving it a lot of thought, and I don't want to miss any of the baby's milestones," he said. "It's time for me to go home with my girls."

At first I thought the doctors would be able to talk him out of that plan; after all, he still had far to go in his recovery, and I couldn't imagine taking care of all his needs myself—much less the baby's on top of them—yet he seemed deaf to their advice. So, with a determination to do what he wanted and an honest belief that God would see me through it, I secured a Hoyer Lift from the VA, which would help Nathan get in and out of bed at home, ordered a shower chair so that I could bathe him without fall risk, and asked Nathan's team to outfit us with our first two weeks' worth of cath kits, ostomy supplies, and wound care dressings. After that, whatever else we needed would be shipped directly to our place.

By the day of Nathan's release, I was a bundle of nerves. And though I hate to admit it, I wasn't eager for him to come home. JoAnn's family medical leave had reached its end, and she had to go back to Alabama. Not only did I need time to adjust to that loss but also the baby's demands before I could focus so much of my limited energy on him. Nevertheless, I took a deep breath, said a long prayer, strapped Eva Blake against my chest, and told myself I could do it, forcing myself to sign his exit paperwork and to say goodbye to our wonderful care team. When I got all three of us Nelsons into our small home and knew that whatever anyone needed from that point forward—whether dinner, clean laundry, hygiene help, or continuing wound care—was up to me, however, I felt a fresh wave of debilitating fear. Thoughts of the daily trips we'd be making back to the hospital for ongoing therapy didn't help.

That first day and night served as a fair indicator of what the next months would involve. Almost as soon as I closed the entry door behind us, just after lunch, Nathan needed help getting out of his chair and into the bed. Just before we'd left, the doctor had advised that he stay out of the wheelchair as much as possible because of the deep tissue injuries on the back of his heels. Each was the size of a half dollar and looked like a nasty purple bruise with a burst blister in the middle. As I got him settled in our bed, with Eva strapped to my back, I realized that both of those holes were draining fluid through the bandages and socks. Already it was time to change the dressings.

As I went on a quick dig to find the supplies I needed, I could feel Eva's diaper warming and filling against the small of my back. So I paused in what I was doing to care for her and also made a bottle. Minutes later, I handed her to Nathan so he could feed her while I packed the wounds on his feet. It was hard to keep a straight face as the awful injuries were exposed, and I hoped that Nathan would be so focused on Eva Blake that he wouldn't see the distress in my eyes. The wound odor was putrid, like rotting garbage.

The next hours involved Daddy and daughter naps as well as further bladder and bowel care for two, not to mention taking Barkley out. I also emptied Nathan's luggage from the hospital, putting away clothing and deciding where all of his care items should live. When that was done, I popped a frozen pizza in the oven for dinner. While it baked, I bathed Eva Blake in a sink and put her in a onesie before helping Nathan into nightclothes. When the kitchen timer sounded, the race was on to slice, serve, and eat the meal before it grew cold. No sooner had I put the last of our dishes into sudsy water than the baby needed to eat again. And Barkley wanted to play.

By the time my head hit the pillow that night, I was so tired it hurt to move. And my stomach growled because I'd been so distracted with my family's needs that I'd barely eaten my pizza. The good news was that I had at least managed a shower, which helped me relax a bit. I'm embarrassed to admit that eight days would pass before I'd find time for another.

Two hours after I fell into that first exhausted sleep, my alarm buzzed. It was time to get up and turn Nathan, whose forced inactivity left him prone to developing new bed sores beyond those we'd already weathered at the hospital. I gave him his required meds, replaced his catheter bag, and again changed the bandages on his heels before drifting fitfully to Dreamland again. Two hours later, I repeated the steps of nighttime care and made a sandwich and glass of milk for Nathan, who tended to wake up hungry. Then, not quite two hours after that, I did it all again. And fed and changed Eva. What a tremendous blessing it was that from the first week of her little life, she'd soundly sleep for six hour stretches at night!

Such became my new pattern of existence. And while Nathan and I were genuinely pleased to have one another close and to get a break from all of the constant intrusion that is part of hospital life, we both dropped weight rapidly. Not only was it hard to cook sufficient meals to keep up with the kind of high calorie demands we both needed in those days, but I often struggled to find time to eat. By the day Eva Blake was three months old, I'd lost more than all of my baby weight and was beginning to look gaunt and gray.

"Pull it together, Jen," I coached myself one morning as I sat in the bathroom and tried to summon the strength to face a new Monday. I'd nearly had a panic attack when I caught a good glimpse of the old lady staring back at me from my mirror. "Your legs and hands still work. You haven't lost seventy pounds of muscle mass due to atrophy. No feeling sorry for yourself. You've no time for that. Things will get better. They will."

Honestly, things did seem to go a little smoother that day. I didn't find any new pressure wounds on Nathan. I ordered dinner in. And I spent quite a bit of time sitting in the floor and playing with Eva as she kicked her chubby feet in the air and made happy baby sounds. Entertaining Eva was always the most fun thing I did in a day.

Only a few months later, however—months of the same old struggles plus the added exhaustion of chasing my fast-growing crawler, I was ready to admit I needed some emotional help.

When an old friend called to check on Nathan, I let my guard down and told her that while he was doing well overall, I was feeling worn out. Headed toward depression. "Come on, Jen," was her immediate reply, "you have nothing to complain about. Nathan's home and recovering just like you wanted. You're fine. You've just got to remember that he is much worse off than you. Do that and it'll all be okay."

She might just as well have dumped ice water on a woman dying of hypothermia.

I cried quietly when that awful call ended. "God, please help me down here," I prayed brokenly. "I'm really struggling." While I didn't receive an answer just then, it made me feel better to remember that no one knew better than He that my admission to our family friend was not a cry for pity but a plea for help.

In time I would learn that my problem had a name: care giver burnout. It's a condition in which a person gets so exhausted by tending everyone else's needs while taking little time for her own that physical, mental, and emotional exhaustion threaten to shut her down. It's certainly not abnormal, nor is it something to feel guilty about. Moreover, it is a preventable condition—when others will step up to lessen the care giver's daily load occasionally.

In those early days post hospital life, I really didn't have much help. And I couldn't afford to hire any. We didn't have family in Tampa, and there wasn't much any of them could do for me over the phone. Troublesome too was the reality that it was impossible for us to get out and make friends outside those at the VA. And in the few times people did call to check on Nathan, they seldom asked whether they could send us a gift card to help with groceries or meals, or to do a mental checkup on me. While I was very much the soldier under fire in those days, he was the only soldier most people considered.

Aid for me finally arrived when the Lord prompted my heart to look into counseling. I made some calls and discovered that I could see a family therapist at the VA while Nathan was in physical therapy: the cost of this would be covered since Nathan was receiving treatment on site. The counselor's background provided her with understanding of veterans, caregivers, and post injury complications, and she assured me that they had a box of baby-safe toys with which Eva could play while we talked.

I went to the initial session and quickly discovered that for the first time in a long time, I could speak openly and candidly with another person about all the unending hurdles I'd had to jump since that rocket blast. And I didn't have to feel ashamed of my feelings or fear judgment for any admission. Every session, in fact, left me feeling better prepared to handle the next hurdle. "You're a power girl, honey, who is raising a power girl," she would say to me as I left each time. Going to her for counsel marked a huge turning point in my life. I was combatting secondary post traumatic stress disorder on top of a tribulation of spiritual warfare.

One of my favorite things about that therapist was that she was a Godly woman who knew how to help me keep my difficult journey in right perspective. To view it as a God-appointed mission that He was not only helping me through incrementally but that He would eventually use in ways I couldn't imagine.

After I got that, I stopped being so bothered by the complications of my life or by what people didn't think to step in to do. I began to be a lot more grateful for even the littlest things. To welcome the occasional care package from a friend as a box of love, particularly when I opened it to find that an encouraging verse of Scripture had been placed perfectly right on top. Things like that were never pushed to the side or looked past. In fact, they often helped me get through one more day, one more week. To stay in the trenches and fight for my little family, trusting that God really did have plans for us beyond the months of intense struggle and running back and forth to the hospital—even in that awful season when Nathan's deep tissue injuries got so much worse that he had to be readmitted temporarily. (While I had done everything right in doctoring his heels, Nathan's refusal to do his in-home therapy faithfully caught up with him—a setback which he loathed.)

Nevertheless, by the time Eva Blake was six months old, and her "Dah" had become her favorite person and was back at home with some consistency, Nathan began to make some breaks toward independence that helped me see there really might be light at the end of our difficult tunnel. First, he started to fold basketfuls of laundry when I set them on the bed beside him. He was slow at it, but he could do it. (Any housekeeping help was major in those days.) Next, he regained the ability to stand upright, which would aid him in the fight against bone density loss and further atrophy issues. During his visits to the hospital, his therapist strapped him—chest, hips, knees, and ankles—to a gurney-like table that could be raised incrementally so he could spend time in an upright position. This couldn't repair his spinal cord, or make him walk, but it absolutely helped him to see that after a time of few gains, further big wins were possible if he'd keep pushing for them. (For long months, it had made him extremely dizzy to be near such a position.) Not long after that, he transitioned into a manually-operated chair that he could power with the recovered strength of his own arms and hands.

Around that same time, he announced to me that he'd been thinking about things a lot lately and had decided that while he hadn't done much to share his faith in Jesus with others prior to injury, he was going to start studying the Bible to gain more confidence in sharing. "Of course, I won't have to know how to answer every question somebody might ask," he said, "but I want to be ready to talk about Christ with others without hesitating. Especially those who are really hurting. I think, in fact, that might be what God wants me to do with everything that's happened."

"Oh?" I asked, pleased to hear the excitement in his voice. It was a nice change. Being so dependent on me was often a real downer for him.

"Absolutely," he said with conviction in his eyes, "I think my obvious injuries just might be a great way to get conversations about matters of faith started."

17
NECESSARY CHANGES

"Do everything in love."
1 Corinthians 16:14

Things continued to improve for our little family, slowly and steadily—yet with just enough setbacks to keep us from taking any win for granted.

One day when Eva Blake was about a year old, the three of us sat in the living room while Nathan and I discussed the need for new quarters. We knew that wherever we went long term, which was the kind of relocation we had in mind that morning, we would need a place geared toward Nathan's needs. A space that could better accommodate all the life accessories necessary for him to function well. Additionally, we were both constantly having to maneuver around Eva Blake's toys: it was time she had her own room. Moreover, Nathan was about to be formally discharged from his ties to the Tampa VA. We had decided to stay in Florida, but there was no need to limit ourselves to the immediate area. By that point we were eager to get away from a place we both associated with struggle.

"You know, we always really enjoyed vacationing in Destin growing up," I said as our daughter set her doll on Nathan's lap and then toddled a few steps away to pick up her favorite bear to place beside it. "EB" adored her daddy. "If we moved there, our families could come see us when they make their beach trips. That would be convenient for everyone. And from what I've read, that area has great schools."

"All that's true," he said, running his hand over Eva Blake's blonde hair as she grinned up at him and patted his knees contentedly. "It's also near Hurlburt Air Force Base. Not a bad work option for me."

My heart soared to hear him speak of working again. His body wasn't yet up to the daily grind of going in to sit in front of a computer all day, but there was nothing wrong with his mind. Already he'd conquered driving our new pickup truck with the help of a specially built hand-operated system the VA installed. And he'd taken on managing our household's finances. What joy and pride I felt every time he took a new stride toward independence, toward truly leading our home.

"Well, then," I said after a minute of thoughtful silence, "I think the best thing to do is apply with Building Homes for Heroes, noting Destin as the place we'd like to be." We already knew from research that a completely wheelchair-accessible house complete with widened doorways and adjusted bath and kitchen features was a rarity—and an incredibly expensive one at that. The organization I mentioned was known for erecting and retrofitting houses for wounded military men and women as well as assisting Gold Star families, the spouses and children of those soldiers killed in action, with houses in which they could rebuild their lives. If anyone could help us, then, they could. And we'd certainly need help: Nathan would need to retire from the Air Force soon, and I hadn't earned a paycheck since I'd left Tacoma. (Thank God for that savings account we'd long worked hard to build!)

Within a month, we submitted our housing application, got Nathan's official discharge paperwork from the VA, and packed up for our new lives in Destin, Florida. Knowing it would be a while before we would hear anything firm from Building Homes for Heroes, we rented a small house and set about doing life in the northwestern panhandle. Things were far from perfect there; nevertheless, being in that new setting among so many old memories from happy vacation days gave me a mental lift.

Although Nathan had made tremendous gains since that fateful day in Afghanistan, had continued to grow in his spiritual resolve, and could drive as well as I could, he fell into an emotional funk not long after the move. Aside from the light housework he'd taken over and playing with Eva Blake while I ran errands, there wasn't much for him to do regularly in Destin. Gone were the routine visits to the VA, the opportunities to prove himself in therapy. And the massive physical exertion that it took for him to go sightseeing anywhere—everything from needing help in getting up and dressed to aid getting his wheelchair in the truck—was a deterrent to exploring on his own. For a time, Nathan usually opted to stay at the house if I didn't insist he do otherwise.

This problem reached a crisis point when I found him lying in our bed one lunchtime, not even responding to my voice when I said his plate was ready and set Eva Blake down beside him. Instead, he just stared morosely at the wall even as she crawled across the mattress and laid down across his chest, rubbing his arm with her little hand as if to offer comfort. *"God, please help me know what to say here,"* I prayed as I parked the lunch tray I'd brought him on the dresser and sat down beside them.

"Nathan, we have to talk," I said.

"What's on your mind?"

"Could you look at me, please?"

He turned his head my way and Eva Blake sat up and patted his chest, clearly pleased to see some signs of interest coming from her beloved Dah.

"Nathan, we are Team Nelson, right?"

He nodded slowly in agreement.

"Yet when you check out like this, I don't feel like we're a team at all."

"I'm sorry, Jen. I'm just so tired all the time. I'll do better."

"This isn't about deciding to do better. I've been praying about this since we moved, and I really think it's time we get you on a rigid schedule. That we stop letting your limitations decide so many things for you and start insisting that your body do all it can—in a rhythm that works better for all of us."

He looked up at me, frowning.

"For starters," I said decisively, "there will be no more lying in bed through meals—unless you're sick. You need to get up with us, every day. And sit at the table and have breakfast with us every day. You need to eat lunch and dinner when we do, too. I know you say you aren't hungry then, but I won't be running to the kitchen to get you a midnight snack on top of everything else anymore. We can keep some protein bars over there on the nightstand for emergencies, but you will be in charge of eating in tandem with me."

He was quiet for a moment, clearly processing. But then he smiled and said, "Nothing with peanut butter."

"Of course not," I said, pleased that he seemed open to my thoughts.

"O cose not," Eva Blake parroted, wrinkling her nose at me and winning a laugh and a hug.

"Also," I said to Nathan as she moved out of my arms and to the end of the bed to play with his unfeeling toes, "I won't be getting up at night anymore just because you are hot or cold. I've just got to get more rest. It'll help all of us."

"I can't help it that I get really hot and then really cold at night, Jen," he protested. "There is no between."

"Then it's time to shop for some blankets better for temperature regulation. I'll look it up today."

This too he seemed to process silently for a moment before offering, "I really like that afghan we have. Helps to keep me at a moderate temp."

I thanked him for that insight and commented on how I would start making sure to cover him with the afghan when we went to bed each night. Then I decided it was time to broach the subject heaviest on my mind. "You are spending far too much time lying prone lately, Nathan. And I really think it's messing with your ability to rest well at night and stay motivated during the day. Not only am I concerned you might get another bed sore, but you need activity."

He sighed. "If you are talking about me using that home gym you set up, know that it isn't that I don't appreciate it. It's just really uncomfortable to work out."

"You know how important stretching and lifting are, babe."

He scowled at me just before Eva Blake sought my help in getting down off the bed so she could play with her toys in the corner beside us. "It's just not the same as before," he sighed.

"There are a lot of things that aren't the same as before. You can't think about the before and expect it to be the now. I don't dwell on it. You can't either."

"But it's humiliating! There was a day when I felt like I could lift anything. Some days now I have a hard time lifting a milk jug."

Hearing the distress in his voice squeezed my heart, but I fought the desire to sympathize and decided to try a new angle. "Nathan, laying around all day unless I coax you to move won't fix anything. It just lets your mind dwell on what was or could have been. A day is fast approaching when our little girl is going to want her daddy to play ball with her. To go eat lunch with her at school. If you want to be ready for those tasks—which I really believe are within your grasp—you are going to have to work toward them daily."

"I can't throw a ball, Jen," he said as he frowned, glassy-eyed, at the ceiling. "For me, it's work even to sit up straight."

I leaned over and kissed his forehead. "But you *can* hold a ball. And you *can* sit up beautifully. And you can do both tasks because you worked hard to earn them."

He fell quiet after that, and I decided to push him just a little further. "So ... how 'bout it?"

Nathan's mouth tightened, his forehead creasing as he loudly exhaled. I held my breath, unsure of what he was thinking. And, oh, what relief I felt to see the corner of his mouth slowly lift in a smirk as his eyes sparked with mischief. He said, "How 'bout you help me get out of this bed, woman? I hear I've got a lunch to eat, and I think I just might let my girls chase me through the park after that."

Things began to change rapidly in our home that very day. A fact for which I still thank the Lord. Not only did we immediately begin implementing the changes discussed, but we both started seeking God for guidance in how to move forward with our lives. To get out of recovery mode and on to doing life again. Out of this rose major shifts.

No sooner had Nathan adjusted to the schedule we made for him than he announced that he was ready for a new challenge. He wanted to go back to work, to take the official steps toward retirement and whatever the future held. "It'll be good for me to get up and put my uniform on each day," he told me as I tried to get excited about starting our day at 5:00 a.m. "I'll gain some new opportunities. Get some more realistic therapy than anything they offered at the VA."

It turned out he was right. And while he never felt like he was much help over at Hulbert, the routine and mental activity he received there proved highly beneficial. He grew confident again, becoming increasingly friendly when we were out in public as a family, and quickly growing more adept at navigating the world outside our home in spite of his challenges. Just seeing the self-respect on his face as he headed off each morning in uniform made my heart race.

Yet one of the best moments from that period happened after a work day—at Walmart, of all places. I had Eva Blake in a shopping cart and Nathan was following along behind us in his wheelchair. When I got to the end of one aisle and prepared to head down the next one, I realized I was no longer hearing the chair's rubber wheels swish and occasionally squeak against the concrete flooring. Puzzled, I paused and turned back. Nathan was speaking with another man, about his age, down near the canned soups.

When we got into the truck a while later to head home, I asked Nathan what he and the stranger had been talking about so earnestly.

"He's an army veteran," Nathan said as he reversed out of our parking space. "Told me it was the first time he'd been out at Walmart during the daytime in years. PTSD."

I winced, knowing Post Traumatic Stress Disorder can leave its sufferers looking whole and healthy on the outside yet potentially more emotionally challenged than Nathan was physically. "Why did he share that, do you think?"

"He recognized me because our paths crossed some years back. Asked what happened to land me in the chair. When I told him, he opened up about the mental demons he has to fight since confronting the Taliban. How his memories make it hard for him to cope with daily tasks."

"I'm sorry," I said as Nathan maneuvered our truck out onto the main road.

"I am too," he agreed. "But you know, as we found common ground through talking about our injuries, I actually got a chance to test out my theory."

"What theory is that?"

"Well, I asked him plainly how his walk with God is going. And he said that while he accepted Jesus into his life as a boy, he's really struggling with how He could allow the trauma he experienced. And I said that while I could certainly understand his feelings on that point, I've found that growing in my relationship with Jesus is one of the best tools I have in dealing with the scars I carried home."

I couldn't believe he'd been so bold. So transparent. That he really had just lived out his dream of one day using his trials to help point others to hope through a relationship with God. "That's wonderful!" I said.

Nathan smiled widely, the corners of his eyes crinkling as his face filled with a sense of purpose I hadn't seen since he'd left for his last deployment three years prior. "The best part is that I got his phone number. Think I'll call to check on him here in a day or two. I'd really like to encourage him further."

18
SEEING GOD'S HAND

"I know the plans I have for you," says the Lord. "They are plans
for good and not for disaster, to give you a future and a hope."
Jeremiah 29:11

I wish I could say that when Nathan and I were dating years ago, I would've gladly agreed to be his life partner even had I known all we would face together. That as a girl I was as iron-willed and mission-focused as I am today. Frankly, it would be wonderful could I confidently report that if I had it to do all over again, I would throw off all fear related to the rocket attack and never once doubt whether I could get through to what I think of as the healed side of things. But the truth is that I only learned how strong I am, how deeply I love my husband, and what my own divine gifts are through walking through all the difficult parts of our journey as they unfolded. By choosing to trust God to see us through them one blind step at a time.

When I began writing this book in early 2015, I did so as a way of getting our family story on paper to hand down to Eva

Blake someday. To help her see that both of her parents are, in a sense, warriors. Warriors who've fought for our marriage and who choose to live as soldiers of Christ rather than victims of circumstances. When I finally shared my early draft with Nathan, however, he mentioned something that I couldn't stop thinking about. He said, "To most people the thought of paralysis at the age of thirty or truly stepping up to be a loved one's caregiver over the long haul sounds daunting. Maybe even a cruel sentence to struggle and suffering. But when you shift your perspective, you start to see how much greater an impact difficult lives can have than simple ones. That injuries and terrible experiences can actually lead to good."

It was this insight that made me think that perhaps in sharing our experiences with those outside our immediate circle, someone in need of that fresh perspective might receive it. (Thus, the resulting volume.)

I admit, though, that when *Captain* Nathan Nelson retired on my birthday, November 28, 2015, I lacked the kind of vantage point I'd need to write for the benefit of a wider audience. And while Nathan was well on his way to developing his mature stance on such matters, back then he too sometimes struggled.

We had no idea what would come next for us once we got home from his retirement banquet, and that was more than a little nerve-wracking. The recent news we'd received from Building Homes for Heroes, however, helped us to stay positive while we waited for other answers. They had accepted our application and were starting to build us a mortgage-free forever home right there in Florida's panhandle. It would include everything Nathan would need to feel comfortable and capable there, as well as a few touches that made it reflect my own tastes. Knowing that brick, one-story house was in process was like a wonderful hug of reassurance from the Lord. How grateful we were for all the donors and volunteers who sacrificed to make it possible!

With the affordable housing concern off our shoulders, it was time to ramp up our prayers regarding career direction. Nathan and I were unsure about what kind of work either of us could get back into, and neither of us had any desire to retire from life in general. Though Nathan still had a lot of assistive needs that were my responsibility, he was firm that he didn't just want a job: he wanted purposeful work—work through which he could live out his ever-deepening convictions about helping others. And since Eva Blake was fast approaching the day when she'd start preschool, I knew I would need to find a position that would allow me to work as much or as little as necessary to accommodate whatever Nathan or she would need.

For a long time, "God, what is our mission for growing and supporting the work of Your kingdom?" became our daily prayer. We constantly asked Him to show us His purpose and direction for our family. Yet, for months, the only answer we received was a deep sense that He was working on things and would reveal His plan in His own timing.

Eventually, through a series of events, I started working as a real estate agent in Northwest Florida. While I wasn't sure at first whether it was something I would do forever, I quickly discovered it was a wonderful fit for my get-things-done personality and also offered the kind of flex schedule my family's needs required. In time I began to enjoy selling houses in and around Destin and to excel in it. Helping military families to relocate to our area became one of my favorite things to do. And I even started using my own experiences to teach other military wives how to save money and build up their own nest eggs, in the event they might find themselves walking a journey similar to my own.

A potential lead for Nathan opened up at a Building Homes for Heroes event to which we were invited in 2016. There Florida State Representative Matt Gaetz invited us out to dinner. When we sat down together the following week, he shared with us that there is a whole community of ill and injured service members spanning Northwest Florida. "This group needs to feel welcomed, appreciated, and supported by the state they've chosen to call home," Representative Gaetz said with conviction.

I knew this declaration of love for our nation's military and their families to be sincere when he explained that he'd asked us out to eat specifically because he wanted Nathan's input on what could be done to help them practically. "What do you need?" he asked us. "What changes might our area implement to make it more amenable to the other wounded warriors who settle here?" After an hour of conversation during which Nathan's preliminary ideas were discussed at length, he said, "You have a wonderful way of inspiriting patriotism when you speak, Nathan. If I win the Congressional race for Florida, I want you on my team as the Assistant Director of Military Affairs. Would you consider the role?"

Oh, if only I had a picture of the elated look on Nathan's face when we got home that night! After hearing the representative's plans for the job he'd offered Nathan, and agreeing that we would henceforth call him Matt, we both knew there wasn't a role in the world that would better suit Nathan's strengths. I was so proud of him and delighted for him that it never occurred to me that Matt Gaetz's election was anything less than certain. Thankfully, he did win that November, almost immediately calling to insist that Nathan join him as if he didn't want to do the job without him.

Nathan, of course, accepted the post and quickly learned that the first Congressional District of Florida has a higher concentration of active-duty military citizens than any other district in the nation. It also houses six military installations representing all service branches of the military, and at least sixty percent of the district's economy exists as a result of defense spending. There's no place like it in the whole country.

As of today, Nathan's primary job remains understanding what congressional support the local military mission needs and communicating it to the Congressman in DC, even as he works hard to build relationships with the district's defense contractors who can support that mission. Nathan and a group of like-minded colleagues, Matt Gaetz among them, want to see northwest Florida become known as the most veteran friendly area in the United States. Not only is my man in a position to look for ways to improve the quality of life for veterans and to work toward implementing them, then, but Nathan has the knowledge and access to make the families he encounters aware of government and charitable programs that can benefit them. And—whether he's off the clock or on—he rarely misses a chance to tell about the ultimate hope everyone has through accepting Jesus Christ as Lord.

Since Nathan first began the beautiful dual mission that now occupies so much of his time, I've accompanied him as needed—often traveling with him to various speaking engagements. Over time, he's became a regular speaker at churches in particular, in part because he'll talk for only the cost of a love offering made out to one of our favorite veteran's organizations but also because the testimony he shares is so compelling. Whereas once his greatest ambition was to climb the Air Force ranks to make a name for himself, he now takes pride in elevating the name of Jesus and advocating for veterans of all ranks so that they and their families might reach their full potential. What pride fills my chest when I see him roll himself out onto a stage looking devastatingly handsome in a suit and tie. He sits so tall now, his voice and mind as sharp as ever and his body far more capable than we would have believed back in those hard days at Walter Reed.

Occasionally I am asked whether Nathan or I resent the harsh turn our lives took in Afghanistan on that September day. But while few things in our world are easy even with all the blessings we enjoy, we both realize now that in some ways the messiest parts of our story have completely transformed us for the better. Our marriage, for instance, has grown so much stronger. Our faith is much more deeply rooted. We have a profoundly deeper understanding of who we are as individuals and as a couple, and neither of us struggle anymore with wondering what our purpose is. Often, in fact, Nathan says he would gladly endure all the suffering again to get to the blessings and mission he has on this side of his injuries.

Amazingly, I find that I feel much the same way. I love that selflessness marks my husband's work, that Eva Blake is being raised in a home where the needs of others are regularly considered along with our own. And I find deep satisfaction not only in watching Nathan shine but in doing what I can to support his mission and the work of other likeminded advocates for military families. In 2018 I was named a Dole Caregiver Fellow for the state of Florida, thus officially representing the caregivers of wounded veterans from all service eras and branches in the Sunshine State. Part of that work involves speaking to legislators and lawmakers about the needs and struggles of such individuals and suggesting legislative changes that would pave the way toward a brighter future for America's Hidden Heroes.

Sometimes I think back on the conversations I had with some less-than-supportive doctors and friends in those first days after Nathan was flown home from Afghanistan. Honestly, with the exception of what Dr. Jerk Face had to say, I don't even remember who said what discouraging thing to me. I only know that had I listened to popular opinion and left Nathan in order to pursue a more "normal" life for myself and our baby, I—and so many others who have since been touched by Nathan's compassion and concern for his fellow soldiers—would've missed out. I know for certain that my husband needed me to keep my promises even when doing so was difficult. To help him climb the mountain before him, even when there were moments when he needed to be carried.

It could be that as you've read our story, you find yourself facing a seemingly insurmountable mountain of your own. Perhaps you've been injured in combat, an accident, or through illness, and doctors aren't offering much hope. Or it could be that your spouse, parent, or child is the one who is ill, maimed, or even emotionally challenged, and you are providing round the clock care. No matter the difficulty in your life, please know that no hardship has to have the last word. You are not alone in the fight. You are loved! The same God who made us does not waste our pain when we ask Him to use it. If you'll turn to Him for help, He will—in time—bring blessings that you, and likely others, would never want to miss. It's my sincere belief that *you* too, dear friend, can face anything. Not as a victim of circumstances, but as a *Divine Soldier* on mission to make our broken world a better place.

May a day come when you look back on whatever you are facing in this season with a perspective that says, "My journey certainly required some unexpected climbs, patience, and perseverance; nevertheless, the view from the top was absolutely worth it."

The Real Nelson's

Nathan tied that sweet mans tie in Chicago, 2008

We got married in February 2009

Nathan Graduates OTS, 2011

Welcoming Nathan home from his second tour, 2011, Tacoma Washington.

and

Below, Nathan, Barkley, I at Mount Rainier State Park 2012

June 2013, Nathan and I with the family in Orange Beach, AL.
Pre-deployment vacation, I was 3 months pregnant with Eva

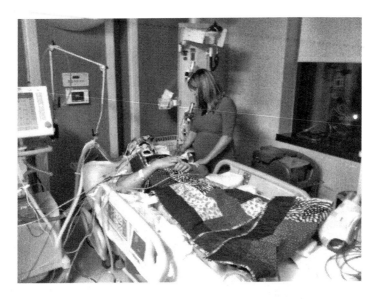

Above: The first time post injury I saw him, September 2013

Below: When Nathan woke up two weeks later

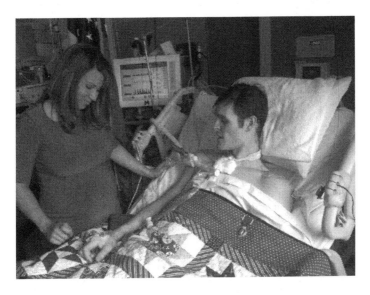

(I re-wore that dress for him)

Above: Nathan and Tom Nelson before Nate's therapy began, 2013

Eva and Nathan took lots of naps together, Eva is 1 week old
December 2013

Eva at 4 months old hanging with dad in therapy, 2014

Nathan and Eamon, 2018

Colin, Nathan, and Chandler, 2018

Nathan and Jennifer, Capital Hill Washington D.C. 2017
Advocating for veterans and caregivers

Nathan, Eva, and I at Fort Pickens, Pensacola, FL
2018

Eva, 5, and I, 2019, Dad was on a business trip.

ABOUT THE AUTHOR

Jennifer Nelson resides in Santa Rosa Beach, FL with her husband and their daughter Eva. They continue to soldier on to this very day and are thankful for a life full of rich blessings and opportunities.

The Nelson's celebrated 10 years of marriage in February 2019, as of September 2019 they will celebrate Nathan's 6th Alive Day, which is a day they commemorate as a joyous occasion of how far they have come. Eva will turn 6 in December and continues to shine light into their everyday lives.

Jennifer Nelson was recognized for her advocacy efforts in 2018 when she was appointed the Elizabeth Dole Foundation's Dole Caregiver Fellow for the state of Florida. In this role Jennifer helps to advocate for caregivers from all service branches and eras to find gainful employment or education in the post injury life. In addition to championing positive legislation in Florida's capital hill or in Washington D.C. alongside her husband.

She currently works as an award winning realtor in the Emerald Coast of Florida.

Jennifer continues to champion her husbands successes. Together they champion faith based veteran and caregiver organizations and research that will benefit the lives of future veteran families around the nation.

Nathan and Jennifer have been active public speakers that vocalize their testimonies and how putting God first in their lives and marriage has continued to create blessings and opportunities for them after the struggle.

"We just want people to know that no matter where you are in your life or spiritual walk, God is listening and will provide the guidance that you need right where you are," Jennifer Nelson.

Choosing joy is a choice. They choose it everyday.

Acknowledgements

My husband Nathan and I would like to thank our Savior Jesus Christ, our friends and family, the staff at Walter Reed Hospital, the volunteers and supporters at The Fisher House, and our friends, nurses, staff, and therapists at James A. Haley Veterans' Hospital. Without their help and support, our story would've turned out differently.

Our gratitude also extends to Congressman Matt Gaetz, for his friendship and support. We are grateful to Deanna and Clebe McClary, for encouraging this book idea and for being incredible mentors and friends. Thanks also goes to Kaye Creasman, AFSOC Wounded Warrior Program Manager, and Sandy Simentelli for serving as a backbone to our success and for helping us better understand the source of encouragement and empowerment.

Damon and Dayna Friedman, your friendship, encouragement, and mentorship mean a lot. Ken and Liz Korkow, that you took us under your wings and helped us soar through the help of your spiritual guidance and leadership, as well as the gift of fellowship, have meant more than we can express. Andy and Esther Pujol, our Building Homes for Heroes Family is like a legion of angels on earth who have changed our lives in ways we never anticipated. Your positivity, a bright shining beacon in our lives, is so appreciated. We love you and deeply appreciate you adopting us into the BHH family.

To the 7th Special Forces Operations Group, the 720th Special Operations Group, and the 22nd Special Tactics Operations we say, without you Nathan's life story would've had a much different ending. Thank you for your willingness to go the distance, to do the unthinkable, and to sacrifice selflessly when the mission calls for it. You, too, are like guardian angels to us; you have done more than anyone will know this side of heaven.

Also, we would like to extend appreciation to The Elizabeth Dole Foundation, Korkow Ranch Missions, Semper Fi Fund/America's Fund, Helping our Military Heroes, and Shield of Faith Missions. All of these groups have embraced our family and allowed us to help others fighting the war at home.

Additionally, we would like to thank everyone in our tribe that was mentioned throughout the book. You have offered emotional and spiritual strength through the years, which means more to us than you will ever know. We are lucky to have you!

And last but not least, Bethany McShurley of Faith-Based Editorial Services in Hendersonville, Tennessee, you are a rock star! "Thank you" does not begin to cover the immense value you've added to this book in the contributions you've made. You organized and focused a bundle of words and thoughts from my years of journal entries into a good read. (I am beyond grateful for having been introduced to you, Bethany. What a joy to feel God's guiding hand helping us to ready this book for the printer!)

52409214R00127

Made in the USA
San Bernardino, CA
07 September 2019